CONTENTS

Page

USING THIS GUIDE

LOOKING FOR A MARINA

A MARINA BERTH is defined as a pontoon, quay or river berth where it is possible to walk ashore at all states of the tide.
COASTAL MARINAS are in geographical order around the UK.
INLAND MARINAS are grouped alphabetically in rivers within each geographical section.
Maximum length is recorded in metres.

FRENCH MARINAS for the north French coast from Calais to Brest, are in geographical order.

PRICES

UK PRICES include VAT
Annual berthing fees are recorded as cost per metre based on a 9.1 metre (30 foot) craft. Overnight berthing fees are recorded as cost per metre based on a 9.1 metre (30 foot) craft.

FRENCH PRICES include local tax
Price banding is very common and fees for both overnight and annual berthing are recorded for a 9.1 metre (30 foot) boat. Electricity is not normally charged seperately.

TIDAL ACCESS

Where appropriate, the length of tidal access is included for both UK and French coastal marinas.

FACILITIES FOR PEOPLE WITH DISABILITIES

The ♿ symbol in the guide indicates the marina may have facilities to help certain types of disability. Please contact the marina before arrival to confirm.

Whilst every effort has been made to ensure the accuracy of information in this booklet, the RYA cannot be held responsible for the consequences of any errors that might arise. These details were believed to be correct at the time of printing but may have changed since.

BERTH HOLDERS ASSOCIATIONS

The ☺ sign indicates marinas with an active Berth Holders' Association.
They work closely with marina operators suggesting and discussing ideas for providing better value for money from existing facilities and services.
Examples of benefits include:

• *encouraging the marina to adopt the RYA Berth Holders' Charter*
• *improving marina security by introducing Pontoon Watch schemes*
• *local supplier discounts for association members*
• *organising social events - cruises, lectures, safety demonstrations*
• *helping prioritise improvements to facilities*

THE BERTH HOLDERS' CHARTER

The ➾ sign indicates marinas awarded the RYA Berth Holders' Charter.

The Charter features a set of service standards which any UK marina, irrespective of size or facilities, can deliver. They cover the issues of most concern to marina berth holders.

Marinas awarded the RYA's Berth Holders' Charter are expected to consistently deliver:

VALUE FOR MONEY
• *facilities and services commensurate with fees*
• *a written management policy on customer satisfaction*

SECURITY
• *protection from thieves*
• *prevention of improper access*
• *emergency help always readily available*

FACILITIES
• *suitable for the purpose and competently staffed*
• *adequate in number and readily available*

MAINTENANCE
• *safe, clean facilities maintained in good working order*

SUGGESTIONS AND COMPLAINTS
• *a simple procedure for receiving suggestions and complaints*
• *a prompt effective response and feedback of results*

STAFF
• *available, competent, helpful and with authority to act quickly*

PEACEFUL ENJOYMENT
• *freedom from noisy, disorderly elements, harassment and nuisance*

COMMUNICATION
• *advance information on changes to facilities, conditions, charges, services*

SAFETY
• *effective action for the safety of people and property*
• *implementation of the requirements of Health and Safety legislation*

A number of marinas already meet these requirements. The RYA is keen to encourage every marina, whatever its size or facilities, to include these important issues in their everyday operating standards.

APPLYING FOR CHARTER RECOGNITION
If you would like to receive an information pack on how the RYA Berth Holders Charter could be adopted at your marina please contact

Peter Waring RYA Berth Holders Association Co-ordinator
Telephone: 01825 732345
Fax: 01825 732995

RYA BERTH HOLDER CHARTER HOLDERS

The following marinas have been awarded the RYA Berth Holders' Charter:

PORT SOLENT MARINA

CHICHESTER MARINA

SOVEREIGN HARBOUR MARINA

DOVER MARINA

HAFAN PWLLHELI

Index of UK Marinas

Fleetwood Harbour Village Marina	33	Lymington Marina Ltd	14
Fox's Marina Ipswich Ltd	27	Lymington Yacht Haven	14
Froud's Bridge Marina	45	Lymm Marina	40
Gillingham Marina	24	Malpas Marine	8
Glasson Basin Yacht Co Ltd	33	Maryport Marina	34
Gloucester Docks	60	Mayflower International Marina	9
H J Phillips Boatbuilders	22	Medway Bridge Marina	24
Hafan Pwllheli Marina	35	Medway Pier Marine Ltd	24
Halcon Marine Ltd	25	Meeching Boats	22
Hamble Point Marina	16	Melfort Pier & Harbour	30
Hamble River Boatyard	17	Mercury Yacht Harbour	16
Hamble Yacht Services Ltd	16	Milford Marina	35
Hambleden Mill Marina	50	Mill Marina	57
Harefield Marina	65	Millbay Marina Village	9
Harleyford Estate Ltd	50	Milton Keynes Marina	65
Hartford Marina	55	Mitchell's Boatyard	12
Hartlepool Marina	28	Moodys Swanwick Marina	17
Haslar Marina	18	Mylor Yacht Harbour Ltd	8
Hermitage Marina	55	Naburn Marina Ltd	42
Highway Marine Ltd	45	Napton Marina	46
Hilperton Marina	60	Neptune Marina Ipswich	27
Hole Farm Moorings	47	New Mills Wharf	44
Hoo Marina	24	Newark Marina	42
Horning Ferry Marina	57	Newhaven Marina Ltd	21
Hull Marina	28	Neyland Yacht Haven	35
Humber Cruising Association Ltd	29	Nimbus Narrow Boats	67
Hythe Marina Village	15	Northney Marina	19
Iron Wharf Boatyard	23	Noss-on-Dart Marina	10
Island Harbour	15	Nottingham Castle Marina	64
Isleham Marina Ltd	57	Oban Yachts & Marine Services Ltd	30
James Mayor & Co Ltd	34	Ocean Village Marina	15
Kemps Quay	47	Oundle Marina	58
Kinnego Marina	70	Padstow Harbour	8
Kip Marina	31	Penarth Marina	36
L H Jones & Son	55	Penton Hook Marina	50
L R Harris & Son	66	Peterhead Bay Marina	30
La Collette Yacht Basin	38	Plymouth Yacht Haven	10
Lady Bee Marina	21	Port Dinorwic Marina	35
Largs Yacht Haven	32	Port Edgar Marina	30
Lee Valley Marina - Springfield	47	Port Hamble Marina	16
Lee Valley Marina (Stnstd Abt)	47	Port Medway Marina	48
Lincoln Marina	58	Port Solent Marina	18
Littlehampton Marina Ltd	21	Portavon Marina	61
Liverpool Marina	33	Preston Brook Marina	41
Loch Lomond Marina	70	Preston Marina	33
Longman Yacht Haven	30	Priory Marina Ltd	56

Pyrford Marina Walton Marine Sales	53	Sutton Harbour Marina	9
Quay West Marina	13	Swale Marina	53
Queen Anne's Battery Marina	10	Swansea Marina	36
Racecourse Yacht Basin	50	Taplow Investments Ltd	53
Ramsgate Royal Harbour Marina	23	Tarbert Harbour	31
Red Hill Marina	67	Temple Marina	51
Rhu Marina Ltd	31	Tewkesbury Marina	62
Ridge Wharf Yacht Centre	13	Thames & Kennet Marina	51
River Mill Marina	56	Thames (Ditton) Marina	52
Riverside Lechlade Marina	51	The Gosport Marina Ltd	18
Riverside Marine	21	The Hayling Yacht Co Ltd	19
Ryde Harbour	17	Thornham Marina	20
Rye Yacht Centre	22	Tidemill Yacht Harbour Ltd	29
Salterns Marina	12	Titchmarsh Marina Ltd	26
Saltford Marina	61	Tollesbury Marina	26
Sankey Marine	61	Tollesbury Saltings Ltd	26
Sawley Marina Ltd	42	Torpoint Yacht Harbour	9
Seaborne Yacht Co Ltd	62	Torquay Marina	11
Seaport Marina	69	Town Quay Marina	15
Seatons Marina	37	Troon Yacht Haven	32
Severn Valley Boat Centre	62	Twenty Pence Marina	56
Shamrock Quay	16	Twyford Bridge Marina	48
Shardlow Marina	43	UK Sailing Academy	14
Shepperton Marina Ltd	51	Universal Marina	17
Ship & Anchor Marina	46	Uphill Boat Centre	8
Shobnall Marina	68	Upton Marina	62
Shotley Marina Ltd	27	Val Wyatt Marine - Willow Marina	52
Sileby Mill Boatyard	67	Victoria Marina	38
South Dock Marina	51	Walton Marina	52
South Ferriby Marina	28	Waveney River Centre	58
Southdown Marina	9	Welton Hythe Marina	66
Southsea Marina	19	West Wick Marina Ltd	25
Sovereign Harbour Marina Ltd	22	Westview Marina	56
Sowerby Bridge Canal Basin	41	Weymouth Marina	11
Sparkes Yacht Harbour	19	Weymouth Old Harbour	11
St Helier Marina	38	Whilton Marina Ltd	66
St Katharine Haven Ltd	25	Whitby Marina	28
St Neots Marina	56	White Bear Marina	41
St Peter Port Marinas	38	Willowbridge Marina	66
St Peters Marina	43	Windermere Aquatic Ltd	44
Staniland of Thorne Marina Ltd	43	Windermere Marina Village	41
Stanley Ferry Marina	40	Windsor Marina	52
Stourport Marina	62	Woolverstone Marina	27
Stratford Marina Ltd	63	Youngboats	23
Suffolk Yacht Harbour	27		
Sunderland Marina	28		

1.1 Coastal - South West

Within this section marinas are listed in geographical order from Weston-super-Mare to Christchurch

Uphill Boat Centre

Uphill Wharf	Annual cost per metre:	£60.44
Weston-super-Mare	Overnight cost per metre:	£0.60
North Somerset	Number of berths:	50
Avon	Maximum length:	15
BS23 4XR	Tidal access:	HW±3
tel 01934 418617		

Facilities: WC ⌐ ✗ ⊡D ⧸N ⊗N ⊠ 工 ⛁ ⛁c 🔄 🚗 ⌁v

Padstow Harbour

Padstow Harbour Commissioners	Annual cost per metre:	£n/a
Harbour Office	Overnight cost per metre:	£1.00
Padstow	Number of berths:	80
Cornwall	Maximum length:	40
PL28 8AQ	Tidal access:	HW±2
tel 01841 532239		

Facilities: WC ⌐ ☎ VHF ✗ ⊡D ⊡P ⧸P ⧸N ⊗P ⊗N ⊠ 工 ⛁ ⬜ ⛁c 🔄 ⌁v ⊡ ♿

Falmouth Marina

North Parade	Annual cost per metre:	£229.00
Falmouth	Number of berths:	350
Cornwall	Overnight cost per metre:	£1.60
TR11 2TD	Maximum length:	30
tel 01326 316620	Tidal access:	All states

Facilities: WC ⌐ ☎ VHF ✗ ⊡D ⧸P ⧸N ⊗P ⊗N 工 ⚓ ⛁ ⬜ ⛁c ✂ 🔄 🚗 ⌁v ⊡ ♿

Malpas Marine

Malpas Marine	Annual cost per metre:	£95.00
Maplas	Overnight cost per metre:	£c/m
Truro	Number of berths:	27
Cornwall	Maximum length:	c/m
TR1 1SQ	Tidal access:	HW±3
tel 01872 71260		

Facilities: WC ⌐ VHF ⊡D ⧸P ⊗P 工 ⛁ ⛁c 🔄

Mylor Yacht Harbour Ltd

Mylor	Annual cost per metre:	£144.00
Falmouth	Overnight cost per metre:	£1.50
Cornwall	Number of berths:	25
TR11 5UF	Maximum length:	22
tel 01326 372121	Tidal access:	All states

Facilities: WC ⌐ ☎ VHF ✗ ⊡D ⊡P ⧸P ⧸N ⊗P ⊗N ! ⊠ 工 ⬜ ⛁c 🔄 🚗 ⌁v ⊡ ♿

Torpoint Yacht Harbour

Marine Drive	Annual cost per metre:	£159.00
Torpoint	Overnight cost per metre:	£1.51
Cornwall	Number of berths:	70
PL11 2EH	Maximum length:	12
tel 01752 813658	Tidal access:	All states

Facilities: [WC] 🏠 ☎ ✂ ⛽D ⚓P ♿P ⛴ 🅃 🧺 🍺 🛒c ✂ 🚗 ⚓

Southdown Marina

Southdown Quay	Annual cost per metre:	£146.87
Millbrook	Overnight cost per metre:	£1.02
Torpoint	Number of berths:	70
Cornwall	Maximum length:	50
PL10 1HG	Tidal access:	HW±5
tel 01752 823084		

Facilities: [WC] 🏠 ☎ VHF ✂ ⚓P ⚓N ♿P ⛴ 🅃 🧺 🛒c 🔌 🚗 ⚓ 🅾

Mayflower International Marina

Ocean Quay	Annual cost per metre:	£204.58
Richmond Walk	Overnight cost per metre:	£1.90
Plymouth	Number of berths:	350
Devon	Maximum length:	30
PL1 4LS	Tidal access:	All states
tel 01752 556633		

Facilities: [WC] 🏠 ☎ VHF ✂ ⛽D ⛽P ⚓P ⚓N♿P ♿N ⛴ 🅃 ⚓ 🧺 🍺 🛒c ✂ 🔌 🚗 ⚓ 🅾 ♿

Millbay Marina Village

Millbay Marina Village Management Co Ltd	Annual cost per metre:	£c/m
Great Western Road	Overnight cost per metre:	£c/m
Millbay Docks	Number of berths:	85
Plymouth, Devon	Maximum length:	14
PL1 3EQ	Tidal access:	All states
tel 01752 226785		

Facilities: ☺ [WC] 🏠 VHF ⚓P ♿P ⚓ 🧺 🚗

Sutton Harbour Marina

North Quay House	Annual cost per metre:	£203.53
Sutton Harbour	Overnight cost per metre:	£1.89
Plymouth	Number of berths:	250
Devon	Maximum length:	23
PL4 0RA	Tidal access:	All states
tel 01752 204186		

Facilities: [WC] 🏠 ☎ VHF ✂ ⛽D ⛽P ⚓P ♿P ⛴ 🅃 🧺 🍺 🛒c ✂ 🔌 🚗 ⚓ 🅾

Queen Anne's Battery Marina

Queen Anne's Battery
Plymouth
Devon
PL4 0LP
tel 01752 671142

Annual cost per metre:	£210.00
Overnight cost per metre:	£1.80
Number of berths:	260
Maximum length:	19
Tidal access:	All states

Facilities: ☺ 🚾 🕵 (VHF ⚓ ⛽D ⛽P ✎P ✎N ⊗P ⊗N ⚓ ⚓ 🛒 ⛴ 🛒c ✂ 🔧 🚗 ⬆v ▣

Plymouth Yacht Haven

Shaw Way
Mount Batten
Plymouth
Devon
PL9 9XH
tel 01752 404231

Annual cost per metre:	£170.38
Overnight cost per metre:	£1.35
Number of berths:	450
Maximum length:	45
Tidal access:	All states

Facilities: 🚾 🕵 (VHF ⚓ ⛽D ✎P ⊗P ⚓ ⛴ 🛒 ⛴ 🛒c ✂ 🔧 🚗 ⬆v ▣ ♿

Clovelly Bay Marina (Plymouth)

The Quay
Turnchapel
Plymouth
Devon
PL9 9TF
tel 01752 404231

Annual cost per metre:	£145.00
Overnight cost per metre:	£2.37
Number of berths:	180
Maximum length:	c/m
Tidal access:	All states

Facilities: 🚾 🕵 (VHF ⚓ ⛽D ✎P ✎N ⊗P ⊗N ⚓ ⛴ ⚓ 🛒 ⛴ 🛒c ✂ 🔧 🚗 ⬆v ▣

Dart Marina

Sandquay
Dartmouth
Devon
TQ6 9PH
tel 01803 833351

Annual cost per metre:	£411.25
Overnight cost per metre:	£2.94
Number of berths:	110
Maximum length:	20
Tidal access:	All states

Facilities: 🚾 🕵 (VHF ⚓ ⛽D ✎P ✎N ⊗P ⊗N ! ⚓ ⛴ ⚓ 🛒 ⛴ 🔧 🚗 ⬆v ▣ ♿

Noss-on-Dart Marina

Noss
Dartmouth
Devon
TQ6 0EA
tel 01803 833351

Annual cost per metre:	£258.50
Overnight cost per metre:	£1.29
Number of berths:	180
Maximum length:	20
Tidal access:	All states

Facilities: 🚾 🕵 (VHF ⚓ ✎P ✎N ⊗P ⊗N ⚓ ⛴ ⚓ 🛒 🛒c 🔧 🚗 ⬆v ▣ ♿

Darthaven Marina Ltd

Brixham Road
Kingswear
Dartmouth
Devon
TQ6 0SG
tel 01803 752545

Annual cost per metre:	£276.12
Overnight cost per metre:	£1.65
Number of berths:	270
Maximum length:	20
Tidal access:	All states

Facilities: ▨ ⌂ ☎ VHF ⚓P ⚓N ⊗P ⊗N ⛴ ⚓ 🛒 🗑 ⚓c ✂ ⛽ 🚗 ⚓ ◉ ♿

Brixham Marina

Marina Developments Ltd
Berryhead Road
Brixham
Devon
TQ5 9BW
tel 01803 882929

Annual cost per metre:	£235.00
Overnight cost per metre:	£1.65
Number of berths:	484
Maximum length:	18
Tidal access:	All states

Facilities: ▨ ⌂ ☎ VHF ⚓ ⛽D ⚓P ⊗P ⚓ 🛒 🗑 ⚓c ✂ ⛽ 🚗 ⚓ ◉ ♿

Torquay Marina

Marina Developments Ltd
Torquay Marina
Torquay
Devon
TQ2 5EQ
tel 01803 214624

Annual cost per metre:	£293.00
Overnight cost per metre:	£2.00
Number of berths:	500
Maximum length:	24
Tidal access:	All states

Facilities: ☺ ▨ ⌂ ☎ VHF ⚓ ⛽D ⛽P ⚓P ⊗P ⚓ ⛴ ⚓ 🛒 🗑 ⚓c ✂ ⛽ 🚗 ⚓ ◉ ♿

Weymouth Marina

70 Commercial Road
Weymouth
Dorset
DT4 8NA
tel 01305 767576

Annual cost per metre:	£240.88
Overnight cost per metre:	£2.06
Number of berths:	234
Maximum length:	25
Tidal access:	All states

Facilities: ▨ ⌂ ☎ VHF ⚓P ⊗P 🛒 🚗 ⚓ ♿

Weymouth Old Harbour

Municipal Offices
North Quay
Weymouth
Dorset
DT4 8TA
tel 01305 206423

Annual cost per metre:	£110.53
Overnight cost per metre:	£1.50
Number of berths:	600
Maximum length:	30
Tidal access:	All states

Facilities: ▨ ⌂ ☎ VHF ⛽D ⚓P ⊗P ⛴ 🛒 🗑 ⚓c ✂ ⛽ ⚓ ◉

Cobb's Quay Marina

Marina Developments Ltd	Annual cost per metre:	£240.00
Cobbs Quay	Overnight cost per metre:	£2.00
Hamworthy Poole	Number of berths:	850
Dorset	Maximum length:	c/m
BH15 4EL	Tidal access:	All states
tel 01202 674299		

Facilities: ☺ 🚾 📻 📞 VHF ⚓ ⛽D ⛽P ⚓P ⚓N ♨P ♨N 🛥 🏛 ⚓ 🛒 🍺 🛒c ✂ 🗺 🚗 📙 ⭕

Davis's Boatyard

Cobbs Quay	Annual cost per metre:	£199.75
Hamworthy	Overnight cost per metre:	£1.41
Poole	Number of berths:	97
Dorset	Maximum length:	12.2
BH15 4EJ	Tidal access:	All states
tel 01202 674349		

Facilities: 🚾 📻 📞 ⚓P ⚓N ♨P ♨N 🛥 🏛 ⚓ 🛒 🛒c 🗺 🚗 📙

Mitchell's Boatyard

Turks Lane	Annual cost per metre:	£205.00
Parkstone	Overnight cost per metre:	£n/a
Poole	Number of berths:	62
Dorset	Maximum length:	9
BH14 8EW	Tidal access:	HW±4
tel 01202 747857		

Facilities: 🚾 📻 📞 ⚓ ⚓N ♨N 🛥 🏛 ⚓ 🛒 🛒c 🗺 🚗

Salterns Marina

40 Salterns Way	Annual cost per metre:	£c/m
Lilliput	Overnight cost per metre:	£c/m
Poole	Number of berths:	300
Dorset	Maximum length:	20
BH14 8JR	Tidal access:	All states
tel 01202 709971		

Facilities: 🚾 📻 📞 VHF ⚓ ⛽D ⛽P ⚓P ⚓N ♨P ♨N ! 🛥 🏛 🛒 🍺 🛒c ✂ 🗺 🚗 📙 ⭕

Arthur Bray's Yard

West Quay House	Annual cost per metre:	£c/m
West Quay Road	Overnight cost per metre:	£c/m
Poole	Number of berths:	110
Dorset	Maximum length:	n/a
BH15 1HT	Tidal access:	All states
tel 01202 676469		

Facilities: 🚾 ⚓P ⚓N ♨P ♨N 🏛 ⚓ 🛒 🚗

Quay West Marina

21-23 West Quay Road
Poole
Dorset
BH15 1HX
tel 01202 381111

Annual cost per metre:	£n/a
Overnight cost per metre:	£2.55
Number of berths:	60
Maximum length:	18.3
Tidal access:	Non tidal

Facilities: ⬚ⁿᶜ 🏴 📞 VHF ✂ ⚓ₚ ⊛ₚ 🛢 🚗

Ridge Wharf Yacht Centre

Ridge
Wareham
Dorset
BH20 5BG
tel 01929 552650

Annual cost per metre:	£115.38
Overnight cost per metre:	£1.12
Number of berths:	165
Maximum length:	14
Tidal access:	HW±5

Facilities: ⬚ⁿᶜ 🏴 📞 ✂ ⛽ᴅ ⛽ₚ ⚓ₚ ⚓ₙ ⊛ₚ ⊛ₙ ⛴ 🏗 🛒 🛒ᶜ ✂ 🖼 🚗 ⚓ ◻

Christchurch Marine Ltd

c/o Rossiter Yachts
Bridge Street
Christchurch
Dorset
BH23 1DZ
tel 01202 483250

Annual cost per metre:	£201.50
Overnight cost per metre:	£1.30
Number of berths:	105
Maximum length:	15.24
Tidal access:	c/m

Facilities: ⬚ⁿᶜ ⛽ᴅ ⚓ₙ ⊛ₙ ⛴ 🏗 🛒 🛒ᶜ 🖼 🚗 ⚓

1.2 Coastal - South

Within this section marinas are listed in geographical order from Lymington to Chichester

Lymington Yacht Haven

King's Saltern Road
Lymington
Hampshire
SO41 3QD
tel 01590 677071

Annual cost per metre:	£352.50
Overnight cost per metre:	£2.00
Number of berths:	575
Maximum length:	30
Tidal access:	All states

Facilities: WC 📷 📞 VHF ⚓ ⛽D ⛽P ⚡P ⚡N 🚿P 🏴 🛒 🍺 🛒c ✂ 🔌 🚗 ⬇v 🅾 ♿

Lymington Marina Ltd

The Shipyard
Bath Road
Lymington
Hampshire
SO41 3YL
tel 01590 673312

Annual cost per metre:	£358.53
Overnight cost per metre:	£2.12
Number of berths:	300
Maximum length:	45.7
Tidal access:	All states

Facilities: WC 📷 📞 VHF ⚓ ⛽D ⛽P ⚡P 🚿P 🚢 🏴 🛒 🍺 🛒c ✂ 🔌 🚗 ⬇v 🅾

Bucklers Hard Yacht Harbour

Harbourmaster's Office
Buckler's Hard Yacht Harbour
Beaulieu
Hampshire
SO42 7XB
tel 01590 616200

Annual cost per metre:	£386.78
Overnight cost per metre:	£2.51
Number of berths:	110
Maximum length:	23.3
Tidal access:	All states

Facilities: WC 📷 📞 ⚓ ⛽D ⛽P ⚡P 🚿P 🚿N 🚢 🏴 🛒 🍺 🛒c ✂ 🔌 🚗 ⬇v 🅾 ♿

Cowes Yacht Haven

Vectis Yard
High Street
Cowes
Isle of Wight
PO31 7BD
tel 01983 299975

Annual cost per metre:	£272.50
Overnight cost per metre:	£2.15
Number of berths:	230
Maximum length:	40
Tidal access:	All states

Facilities: WC 📷 📞 VHF ⚓ ⛽D ⚡P ⚡N 🚿P 🚿N 🏴 ⚓ 🛒 🍺 🛒c ✂ 🔌 🚗 ⬇v 🅾 ♿

UK Sailing Academy

Arctic Road
West Cowes
I o W
PO31 7PQ
tel 01983 294941

Overnight cost per metre:	£1.20
Annual cost per metre:	£c/m
Number of berths:	n/a
Maximum length:	26
Tidal access:	All states

Facilities: WC 📷 📞 VHF ⚓ ⚡P ⚡N 🚿P 🚿N 🚢 🛒 🍺 🛒c ✂ 🚗 ♿

Island Harbour

Mill Lane	Annual cost per metre:	£159.12
Binfield	Overnight cost per metre:	£1.48
Newport	Number of berths:	150
Isle of Wight	Maximum length:	20
PO30 2LA	Tidal access:	HW±3.5
tel 01983 822999		

Facilities: ⬛ ☞ 📞 VHF 🅿D ✈P ♿P ⛵ 🏭 ⚓ 🅿 🛒c 🚗 🚙 ⬇v ⬜

East Cowes Marina

Clarence Road	Annual cost per metre:	£211.50
East Cowes	Overnight cost per metre:	£1.94
Isle of Wight	Number of berths:	200
Hampshire	Maximum length:	30
PO32 6HA	Tidal access:	All states
tel 01983 293983		

Facilities: ☺ ⬛ ☞ 📞 VHF ✈P ♿P 🏭 ⚓ 🛒 🚙 ⬇v

Hythe Marina Village

Lock Office	Annual cost per metre:	£287.00
Shamrock Way	Overnight cost per metre:	£2.00
Hythe, Southampton	Number of berths:	210
Hampshire	Maximum length:	17
SO45 6DY	Tidal access:	All states
tel 01703 207073		

Facilities: ☺ ⬛ ☞ 📞 VHF ⛽ 🅿D 🅿P ✈P ✈N ♿P ♿N ❗ ⛵ 🏭 ⚓ 🛒 🅿 🛒c ✂ 🚗 🚙 ⬇v ⬜ ♿

Town Quay Marina

Marina Reception	Annual cost per metre:	£223.25
Town Quay	Overnight cost per metre:	£2.00
Southampton	Number of berths:	135
Hampshire	Maximum length:	12
SO14 2AQ	Tidal access:	All states
tel 01703 234397		

Facilities: ☺ ⬛ ☞ 📞 VHF ⛽ ✈P ✈N ♿P ♿N 🛒 🚙 ⬇v ⬜ ♿

Ocean Village Marina

2 Channel Way	Annual cost per metre:	£299.00
Canute Rd	Overnight cost per metre:	£2.00
Southampton	Number of berths:	450
Hampshire	Maximum length:	40
SO14 3TG	Tidal access:	All states
tel 01703 229385		

Facilities: ⬛ ☞ 📞 VHF ⛽ ✈P ♿P ⚓ 🛒 🚙 ⬜ ♿

Shamrock Quay

Marina Developments Ltd	Annual cost per metre: £258.50
Shamrock Quay	Overnight cost per metre: £c/m
William Street, Southampton	Number of berths: 250
Hampshire	Maximum length: 60
SO14 5QL	Tidal access: All states
tel 01703 229461	

Facilities: 🔲 ⌖ 📞 VHF ⚓ ⛽P ⛽N ⊗P ⊗N 🏬 ⚓ 🍺 🧺 ✂ 🔄 🚗 ⬇ ⊙

Hamble Point Marina

School Lane	Annual cost per metre: £420.00
Hamble	Overnight cost per metre: £2.10
Southampton	Number of berths: 220
Hampshire	Maximum length: 20
SO31 4NB	Tidal access: All states
tel 01703 452464	

Facilities: ☺ 🔲 ⌖ 📞 VHF ⚓ ⛽D ⛽P ⊗P 🚤 🏬 ⚓ 🛒 🍺 🧺 ✂ 🔄 🚗 ⬇ ♿

Port Hamble Marina

Satchell Lane	Annual cost per metre: £401.00
Hamble	Overnight cost per metre: £2.00
Southampton	Number of berths: 310
Hampshire	Maximum length: 22
SO31 4QD	Tidal access: All states
tel 01703 452741	

Facilities: ☺ 🔲 ⌖ 📞 VHF ⚓ ⛽D ⛽P ⛽P ⊗P 🏬 ⚓ 🛒 🍺 🧺 ✂ 🔄 🚗 ⬇ ⊙ ♿

Hamble Yacht Services Ltd

Port Hamble	Annual cost per metre: £329.00
Satchell Lane	Overnight cost per metre: £1.50
Hamble	Number of berths: 60
Hampshire	Maximum length: 30
SO31 4NN	Tidal access: All states
tel 01703 454111	

Facilities: 🔲 ⌖ 📞 VHF ⚓ ⛽D ⛽P ⛽P ⊗P ⊗N 🚤 🏬 ⚓ 🛒 🍺 🧺 ✂ 🔄 🚗 ⬇ ⊙

Mercury Yacht Harbour

Satchell Lane	Annual cost per metre: £376.00
Hamble	Overnight cost per metre: £2.00
Southampton	Number of berths: n/a
Hampshire	Maximum length: 22
SO31 4HQ	Tidal access: All states
tel 01703 455994	

Facilities: ☺ 🔲 ⌖ 📞 VHF ⚓ ⛽P ⛽N ⊗P ⊗N 🚤 🏬 ⚓ 🍺 🧺 ✂ 🚗 ⬇ ⊙ ♿

Hamble River Boatyard

Bridge Road	Annual cost per metre: £n/a
Swanwick	Overnight cost per metre: £n/a
Southampton	Number of berths: 50
Hampshire	Maximum length: 18
SO31 7EB	Tidal access: All states
tel 01489 583572	

Facilities: 🆆 ℞ ☎ ⚓ ⛽ 🏪 ⚒ ⚓ 🔧 🛒 ✂ 🏧 🚗

Moodys Swanwick Marina

Swanwick Shore Road	Annual cost per metre: £323.00
Swanwick	Overnight cost per metre: £1.80
Southampton	Number of berths: 360
Hampshire	Maximum length: 30
SO31 1ZL	Tidal access: All states
tel 01489 885262	

Facilities: 🆆 ℞ ☎ VHF ⚒ ⛽ ⛽ ⚓ ⚓ ⛽ ⛽ ⚓ ⚓ 🛒 🔧 🏪 ✂ 🏧 🚗 ⚓ 🅾

Universal Marina

Solar Marine Ltd	Annual cost per metre: £c/m
Univeral & Crableck Marina	Overnight cost per metre: £1.64
Sarisbury Green, Southampton	Number of berths: 300
Hampshire	Maximum length: 25
SO31 7ZN	Tidal access: All states
tel 01489 886690	

Facilities: 🆆 ℞ ☎ VHF ⚒ ⚓ ⛽ ⚓ ⚓ 🏪 ✂ 🏧 🚗 ⚓

Ryde Harbour

The Esplanade	Annual cost per metre: £c/m
Ryde	Overnight cost per metre: £c/m
Isle of Wight	Number of berths: 200
PO33 1JA	Maximum length: 20
tel 01983 613879	Tidal access: HW±2

Facilities: 🆆 ℞ ☎ VHF ⛽ ⛽ ⚓ ⛽ ⚓ 🛒 🔧 🏧 🚗 ⚓ 🅾

Bembridge Harbour

Harbour Office	Annual cost per metre: £170.37
St Helens Quay	Overnight cost per metre: £1.40
Ryde	Number of berths: 75
Isle of Wight	Maximum length: 20
PO33 1YS	Tidal access: HW±3
tel 01983 872828	

Facilities: 🆆 ℞ ☎ VHF ⛽ ⚓ ⛽ ⚓ ⚓ ⚓ 🛒 🔧 🏪 ✂ 🏧 🚗 ⚓ 🅾 ♿

Haslar Marina

Haslar Road	Annual cost per metre:	£270.25
Gosport	Overnight cost per metre:	£1.88
Hampshire	Number of berths:	600
PO12 1NU	Maximum length:	50
tel 01705 601201	Tidal access:	All states

Facilities: 🚻 📻 ☎ VHF ⛽ 🔌 ⚡ 🔋 🔌 🛥️ 🧺 🍺 🛒 ✂️ 🏪 🚗 ⚓ ⚓

The Gosport Marina Ltd

Mumby Road	Annual cost per metre:	£279.25
Gosport	Overnight cost per metre:	£1.80
Hampshire	Number of berths:	337
PO12 1AH	Maximum length:	25
tel 01705 524811	Tidal access:	HW±5

Facilities: 😊 🚻 📻 ☎ VHF ⛽ 🔌 🔌 🔋 🔌 ⚡ 🏗️ 🔧 🧺 🍺 🛒 🏪 🚗 ⚓

Fareham Yacht Harbour

Portsmouth Marine Engineering Ltd	Annual cost per metre:	£108.00
Lower Quay	Overnight cost per metre:	£0.55
Fareham	Number of berths:	100
Hampshire	Maximum length:	12
PO16 0PS	Tidal access:	HW±3
tel 01329 288221		

Facilities: 🚻 📻 🔌 🔋 ⚡ 🔌 🏗️ 🧺 🍺 🛒 ✂️ 🏪 🚗

Fareham Marine

Lower Quay	Annual cost per metre:	£108.00
Fareham	Overnight cost per metre:	£n/a
Hants	Number of berths:	45
PO16 0PS	Maximum length:	12
tel 01329 822445	Tidal access:	HW±3

Facilities: 🚻 📻 🔌 🔋 ⚡ 🔌 🏗️ 🧺 🏪 🚗

Port Solent Marina

South Lockside	Annual cost per metre:	£249.00
Port Solent	Overnight cost per metre:	£1.85
Portsmouth	Number of berths:	900
Hampshire	Maximum length:	43
PO6 4TJ	Tidal access:	All states
tel 01705 210765		

Facilities: ✏️ 😊 🚻 📻 ☎ VHF ⛽ 🔌 🔌 🔋 ⚡ 🔌 ! 🏗️ 🔧 🧺 🍺 🏪 ✂️ 🚗 ⚓ 🔲 ♿

Southsea Marina

Fort Cumberland Road	Annual cost per metre: £225.60
Southsea	Overnight cost per metre: £1.47
Hampshire	Number of berths: 320
PO4 9RJ	Maximum length: 15
tel 01705 822719	Tidal access: HW±3

Facilities: WC ⌂ ☏ VHF ⚲ ⛽D ⚓P ⚓N ⊗P ⊗N ⛴ 🛒 🍴 ⚓c ✂ 🏪 🚗 ⚓ 🅾

The Hayling Yacht Co Ltd

Mill Rythe Lane	Annual cost per metre: £132.03
Hayling Island	Overnight cost per metre: £0.68
Hampshire	Number of berths: 116
PO11 0QQ	Maximum length: 18
tel 01705 463592	Tidal access: HW±2.5

Facilities: WC ⌂ ☏ ⛽D ⚓N ⊗P ⊗N ⛴ ⚓ 🛒 🏪c 🏪 🚗 ⚓

Sparkes Yacht Harbour

38 Wittering Road	Annual cost per metre: £246.75
Sandy Point	Overnight cost per metre: £1.88
Hayling Island	Number of berths: 150
Hants	Maximum length: 20
PO11 9SR	Tidal access: All states
tel 01705 463572	

Facilities: WC ⌂ ☏ VHF ⚲ ⛽D ⛽P ⚓P ⚓N ⊗P ⊗N ⛴ ⚓ 🛒 🍴 🏪c ✂ 🏪 🚗 ⚓ 🅾 ♿

Northney Marina

Northney Road	Annual cost per metre: £306.00
Hayling Island	Overnight cost per metre: £1.75
Hampshire	Number of berths: 228
PO11 ONH	Maximum length: 24
tel 01705 466321	Tidal access: All states

Facilities: ☺ WC ⌂ ☏ VHF ⚲ ⛽D ⚓P ⚓N ⊗P ⊗N ⛴ ⚓ 🛒 🏪 ⚓ 🅾

Emsworth Yacht Harbour

Thorney Road	Annual cost per metre: £183.00
Emsworth	Overnight cost per metre: £1.22
Hampshire	Number of berths: 150
PO10 8BP	Maximum length: 12
tel 01243 377727	Tidal access: HW±2.5

Facilities: WC ⌂ ☏ VHF ⛽D ⚓P ⚓N ⊗P ⊗N ⛴ ⚓ 🛒 🏪c ✂ 🏪 ⚓

Thornham Marina

Thornham Lane	Annual cost per metre: £174.00
Prinsted	Overnight cost per metre: £0.74
Emsworth	Number of berths: 55
Hampshire	Maximum length: c/m
PO10 8DD	Tidal access: HW±2
tel 01243 375335	

Facilities: [icons]

Birdham Pool

Birdham	Annual cost per metre: £c/m
Chichester	Overnight cost per metre: £c/m
West Sussex	Number of berths: 23
PO20 7BG	Maximum length: 15
tel 01243 512310	Tidal access: HW±3

Facilities: [icons]

Chichester Marina

Birdham	Annual cost per metre: £185.00
Chichester	Overnight cost per metre: £1.50
West Sussex	Number of berths: 1071
PO20 7EJ	Maximum length: 20
tel 01243 512731	Tidal access: HW±5

Facilities: [icons]

Within this section marinas are listed in geographical order from Littlehampton to Ipswich

Littlehampton Marina Ltd

Ferry Road
Littlehampton
West Sussex
BN17 5DS
tel 01903 713553

Annual cost per metre:	£188.00
Overnight cost per metre:	£1.76
Number of berths:	110
Maximum length:	30
Tidal access:	All states

Facilities: 🚾 ☝ ☎ VHF ⚓ ⛽D ⛽P ⚓P ⚓N ⊗P ⊗N ! ⛴ ⚓ ⚓ 🛒 🏪 🏪c 🚃 🚗 ⚓ ⬜

Riverside Marine

The Boathouse
41 Riverside Rd
Shoreham Beach
West Sussex
BN43 5RB
tel 01273 453793

Annual cost per metre:	£c/m
Overnight cost per metre:	£c/m
Number of berths:	10
Maximum length:	c/m
Tidal access:	HW±3

Facilities: ☎ ⚓ ⛽D ⚓P ⚓N ⊗P ⊗N ⛴ ⚓ 🛒 🏪 🏪c ✂ 🚃 🚗

Lady Bee Marina

138-140 Albion Street
Southwick
West Sussex
BN42 4EG
tel 01273 593801

Annual cost per metre:	£167.01
Overnight cost per metre:	£1.81
Number of berths:	140
Maximum length:	150
Tidal access:	HW±5

Facilities: ☺ 🚾 ☝ ☎ VHF ⚓P ⊗P ⛴ 🏪 🏪c 🚃 🚗 ⬛

Brighton Marina

Brighton Marina Moorings Ltd
Marine Trade Centre
Brighton
East Sussex
BN2 5UF
tel 01273 819919

Annual cost per metre:	£217.00
Overnight cost per metre:	£1.90
Number of berths:	1300
Maximum length:	60
Tidal access:	All states

Facilities: 🚾 ☝ ☎ VHF ⚓ ⛽D ⛽P ⚓P ⊗P ! ⚓ ⚓ 🛒 🏪 🏪c ✂ 🚃 🚗 ⬛ ⬜

Newhaven Marina Ltd

The Yacht Harbour
Newhaven
East Sussex
BN9 9BY
tel 01273 513881

Annual cost per metre:	£185.00
Overnight cost per metre:	£c/m
Number of berths:	300
Maximum length:	15
Tidal access:	HW±3

Facilities: 🚾 ☝ ☎ VHF ⛽D ⚓P ⚓N ⊗P ⊗N ⛴ ⚓ ⚓ 🛒 🏪 🏪c 🚃 🚗 ⬛

Meeching Boats

Denton Island	Annual cost per metre:	£59.71
Newhaven	Overnight cost per metre:	£n/a
East Sussex	Number of berths:	90
BN9 9BA	Maximum length:	12
tel 01273 514907	Tidal access:	HW±2

Facilities: 〽N ⊗N ⏏ 🗑 ▣ 🚗

Cantell & Son Ltd

The Old Shipyard	Annual cost per metre:	£16.64
Robinson Road	Overnight cost per metre:	£1.11
Newhaven	Number of berths:	130
East Sussex	Maximum length:	10
BN9 9BL	Tidal access:	HW±2.5
tel 01273 514118		

Facilities: ⓦ ⊗P ⊗N ⏏ ℿ ⟟ 🗑 🗑c ▣ 🚗 ⌊v

Sovereign Harbour Marina Ltd

Pevensey Bay Road	Annual cost per metre:	£186.60
Eastbourne	Overnight cost per metre:	£1.75
East Sussex	Number of berths:	410
BN23 6JH	Maximum length:	20
tel 01323 470099	Tidal access:	All states

Facilities: ✏ ☺ ⓦ 🎣 ☏ VHF ⚓ 🅿D 🅿P 〽P 〽N ⊗P ⊗N ! ℿ ⟟ 🗑 🗄 🗑c ✂ ▣ 🚗 ⌊v ▢ ♿

Rye Yacht Centre

Rock Channel	Annual cost per metre:	£c/m
Rye	Overnight cost per metre:	£c/m
East Sussex	Number of berths:	30
TN31 7HJ	Maximum length:	12.9
tel 01797 225188	Tidal access:	HW±3

Facilities: ⓦ 〽N ⊗N ⟟ 🗑 🚗

H J Phillips Boatbuilders

Rock Channel	Annual cost per metre:	£63.00
Rye	Overnight cost per metre:	£1.11
East Sussex	Number of berths:	20
TN31 7HJ	Maximum length:	15
tel 01797 223234	Tidal access:	HW±2

Facilities: ⓦ 〽P 〽N ⊗N ⏏ ℿ 🗑 ▣ 🚗

Dover Marina

Wellington Dock
Dover
Kent
CT17 9BU
tel 01304 241663

Annual cost per metre:	£c/m
Overnight cost per metre:	£c/m
Number of berths:	358
Maximum length:	50
Tidal access:	All states

Facilities: ⊷ WC 🝔 (VHF ⚲ ⛽D ⚡P ⊗P ⊀ 🕱 ⊥ 🛒 🗐 🗓 🚗 ⬇v ▣ ♿

Ramsgate Royal Harbour Marina

Harbour Offices
Military Road
Ramsgate
Kent
CT11 9LQ
tel 01843 592277

Annual cost per metre:	£164.50
Overnight cost per metre:	£1.50
Number of berths:	400
Maximum length:	100
Tidal access:	HW±2.5

Facilities: ☺ WC 🝔 (VHF ⚲ ⛽D ⛽P ⚡P ⊗P ⊀ 🕱 🛒 🗐 🛒c ✂ 🗓 🚗 ⬇v ▣

Iron Wharf Boatyard

Abbey Fields
Faversham
Kent
ME13 7BT
tel 01795 537122

Annual cost per metre:	£76.00
Overnight cost per metre:	£0.75
Number of berths:	45
Maximum length:	30
Tidal access:	HW±2

Facilities: WC 🝔 (VHF ⛽D ⚡N ⊗N 🕱 🛒 🛒c ✂ 🗓 🚗 ▣

Youngboats

Oare Creek
Faversham
Kent
ME13 7TX
tel 01795 536176

Annual cost per metre:	£88.40
Overnight cost per metre:	£0.55
Number of berths:	120
Maximum length:	12
Tidal access:	HW±1.5

Facilities: WC (⛽D ⚡P ⚡N ⊗P ⊗N 🕱 ⊥ 🛒 🛒c 🗓 🚗 ⬇v

Conyer Marina

Conyer Quay
Teynham
Sittingbourne
Kent
ME9 9HW
tel 01795 521285

Annual cost per metre:	£c/m
Overnight cost per metre:	£c/m
Number of berths:	40
Maximum length:	30
Tidal access:	HW±2.5

Facilities: WC ⚲ ⚡N ⊗N ⊀ 🗐 🗓 🚗 ⬇v

Gillingham Marina

F Parham Ltd	Annual cost per metre: £150.00
173 Pier Road	Overnight cost per metre: £1.40
Gillingham	Number of berths: 500
Kent	Maximum length: 21
ME7 1UB	Tidal access: HW±4.5
tel 01634 280022	

Facilities: [icons]

Medway Pier Marine Ltd

Pier Head Buildings	Annual cost per metre: £95.71
Gillingham Pier	Overnight cost per metre: £0.55
Gillingham	Number of berths: 60
Kent	Maximum length: 14
ME7 1RX	Tidal access: HW±4
tel 01634 851113	

Facilities: [icons]

Medway Bridge Marina

Manor Lane	Annual cost per metre: £c/m
Rochester	Overnight cost per metre: £1.00
Kent	Number of berths: 130
ME1 3HS	Maximum length: 30
tel 01634 843576	Tidal access: HW±5.5

Facilities: [icons]

Cuxton Marina

Station Road	Annual cost per metre: £c/m
Cuxton	Overnight cost per metre: £c/m
Rochester	Number of berths: 90
Kent	Maximum length: c/m
ME2 1AB	Tidal access: HW±5
tel 01634 721941	

Facilities: [icons]

Hoo Marina

Vicarage Lane	Annual cost per metre: £166.85
Hoo	Overnight cost per metre: £1.10
Nr Rochester	Number of berths: 250
Kent	Maximum length: 65
ME3 9LE	Tidal access: HW±3
tel 01634 250311	

Facilities: [icons]

St Katharine Haven Ltd

50 St Katherine's Way	Annual cost per metre:	£220.00
London	Overnight cost per metre:	£1.80
E1 9LB	Number of berths:	200
tel 0171 488 0555	Maximum length:	148
	Tidal access:	HW-2.5+1.5

Facilities: [icons]

West Wick Marina Ltd

Church Road	Annual cost per metre:	£176.25
North Fambridge	Overnight cost per metre:	£c/m
Nr Chelmsford	Number of berths:	180
Essex	Maximum length:	15
CM3 6LR	Tidal access:	HW±5
tel 01621 741268		

Facilities: [icons]

Halcon Marine Ltd

The Point	Annual cost per metre:	£44.50
Canvey Island	Overnight cost per metre:	£0.17
Essex	Number of berths:	300
SS8 7TL	Maximum length:	32
tel 01268 511611	Tidal access:	HW±1.5

Facilities: [icons]

Bridgemarsh Marine

Bridgemarsh Lane	Annual cost per metre:	£c/m
Althorne	Overnight cost per metre:	£n/a
Essex	Number of berths:	150
CM3 6DQ	Maximum length:	n/a
tel 01621 740414	Tidal access:	HW±4

Facilities: [icons]

Burnham Yacht Harbour

Burnham Yacht Harbour Marina Ltd	Annual cost per metre:	£188.00
Burnham-on-Crouch	Overnight cost per metre:	£1.00
Essex	Number of berths:	350
CM0 8BL	Maximum length:	30
tel 01621 782150	Tidal access:	All States

Facilities: [icons]

Blackwater Marina

Marine Parade	Annual cost per metre: £146.83
Maylandsea	Overnight cost per metre: £1.11
Essex	Number of berths: 164
CM3 6AN	Maximum length: 25
tel 01621 740264	Tidal access: HW±2.5

Facilities:

Bradwell Marina

Waterside	Annual cost per metre: £c/m
Bradwell on Sea	Overnight cost per metre: £c/m
Essex	Number of berths: 300
CM0 7RB	Maximum length: 15.25
tel 01621 776391	Tidal access: HW±4

Facilities:

Tollesbury Saltings Ltd

The Sail Lofts	Annual cost per metre: £72.16
Woodrolfe Road	Overnight cost per metre: £0.67
Tollesbury	Number of berths: 120
Essex	Maximum length: 40
CM9 8SE	Tidal access: HW±2.5
tel 01621 868624	

Facilities:

Tollesbury Marina

The Yacht Harbour	Annual cost per metre: £125.00
Tollesbury	Overnight cost per metre: £c/m
Essex	Number of berths: 235
CM9 8SE	Maximum length: 15
tel 01621 869202	Tidal access: HW±2

Facilities:

Titchmarsh Marina Ltd

Coles Lane	Annual cost per metre: £c/m
Kirby Road	Overnight cost per metre: £c/m
Walton-on-Naze	Number of berths: 420
Essex	Maximum length: c/m
CO14 8SL	Tidal access: HW±5
tel 01255 672185	

Facilities:

Shotley Marina Ltd

Shotley Gate	Annual cost per metre:	£210.33
Ipswich	Overnight cost per metre:	£1.53
Suffolk	Number of berths:	350
IP9 1QJ	Maximum length:	25
tel 01473 788982	Tidal access:	All states

Facilities: ⬛ 🧭 📞 VHF ⚓ ⛽ 🅿️ 🅽 ⑄ ⑆ ⚓ ⚓ 🛒 🍺 ☕ 🔧 🚗 ⚓ 🛟 ▣

Woolverstone Marina

Marina Developments Ltd	Annual cost per metre:	£217.00
Woolverstone	Overnight cost per metre:	£1.75
Ipswich	Number of berths:	200
Suffolk	Maximum length:	28
IP9 1AS	Tidal access:	All states
tel 01473 780206		

Facilities: 😊 ⬛ 🧭 📞 VHF ⚓ ⛽ 🅿️ 🅽 ⑄ ⑆ ⚓ ⚓ 🛒 🍺 ☕ ✂️ 🔧 🚗 🛟 ▣

Fox's Marina Ipswich Ltd

The Strand	Annual cost per metre:	£180.40
Wherstead	Overnight cost per metre:	£1.16
Ipswich	Number of berths:	90
Suffolk	Maximum length:	15.5
IP2 8SA	Tidal access:	All states
tel 01473 689111		

Facilities: ⬛ 🧭 📞 VHF ⛽ 🅿️ 🅽 ⑄ ⑆ ⚓ ⚓ 🛒 🍺 ☕ 🔧 🚗 🛟

Neptune Marina Ipswich

Neptune Quay	Annual cost per metre:	£143.00
Ipswich Dock	Overnight cost per metre:	£1.32
Ipswich	Number of berths:	200
Suffolk	Maximum length:	114
IP4 1AX	Tidal access:	HW±2
tel 01473 215204		

Facilities: ⬛ 🧭 VHF ⚓ ⛽ 🅿️ ⑄ ⚓ ⚓ 🛒 🍺 🔧 🚗 🛟

Suffolk Yacht Harbour

Levington	Annual cost per metre:	£191.62
Ipswich	Overnight cost per metre:	£1.23
Suffolk	Number of berths:	500
IP10 0LN	Maximum length:	25
tel 01473 659240	Tidal access:	All states

Facilities: ⬛ 🧭 📞 VHF ⛽ ⛽ 🅿️ 🅽 ⑄ ⑆ ⚓ ⚓ 🛒 🍺 ☕ ✂️ 🔧 🚗 🛟 ▣ ♿

1.4 Coastal - East/North East

Within this section marinas are listed in geographical order from Kingston upon Hull to Ipswich

Hull Marina

Warehouse 13
Kingston Street
Kingston upon Hull
East Yorkshire
HU1 2DQ
tel 01482 613451

Annual cost per metre:	£128.25
Overnight cost per metre:	£1.35
Number of berths:	270
Maximum length:	27.5
Tidal access:	HW±3

Facilities: ☺ 🚾 📻 📞 VHF ⚓ ⛽D ⛽P ✂P ✂N ⊛P ⊛N ! 🏗 🛒 🍺 🛒c ✂ 🚗 ⛴ 🅾 ♿

South Ferriby Marina

South Ferriby
Barton On Humber
North Lincolnshire
DN18 6JH
tel 01652 635620

Annual cost per metre:	£53.00
Overnight cost per metre:	£0.25
Number of berths:	60
Maximum length:	n/a
Tidal access:	HW±3

Facilities: 🚾 📻 📞 VHF ⛽D ✂N ⊛N ! 🏗 ⚓ 🛒 🛒c ⛴

Whitby Marina

Whitby Harbour Office
Pier Road
Whitby
N Yorks
YO21 3PU
tel 01947 602354

Annual cost per metre:	£90.41
Overnight cost per metre:	£1.44
Number of berths:	193
Maximum length:	12.2
Tidal access:	HW±2

Facilities: ☺ 🚾 📻 📞 VHF ⚓ ⛽D ✂P ⊛P ⛴ 🏗 🛒 🛒c 📲 🚗 ⛴ 🅾 ♿

Hartlepool Marina

Lock Office
Slake Terrace
Hartlepool
Teeside
TS24 0RU
tel 01429 865744

Annual cost per metre:	£126.00
Overnight cost per metre:	£1.60
Number of berths:	350
Maximum length:	60
Tidal access:	HW±5

Facilities: 🚾 📻 📞 VHF ⚓ ⛽D ✂P ⊛P ! ⛴ 🏗 ⚓ 🛒 🍺 🛒c ✂ 📲 🚗 ⛴ 🅾

Sunderland Marina

Roker
Sunderland
Tyne & Wear
SR6 0PW
tel 0191 514 4721

Annual cost per metre:	£148.42
Overnight cost per metre:	£1.44
Number of berths:	198
Maximum length:	20
Tidal access:	All states

Facilities: 🚾 📻 📞 VHF ⚓ ⛽D ✂P ⊛P ! ⛴ 🍺 🚗 ⛴ ♿

Amble Marina

Amble
Northumberland
NE65 0YP
tel 01665 712168

Annual cost per metre:	£155.00
Overnight cost per metre:	£1.50
Number of berths:	240
Maximum length:	24
Tidal access:	HW±3.5

Facilities: WC ⬠ ☎ VHF ⚓ 🛢D 🛢P ⚓P ⚓N ⊗P ⊗N ⛴ ⛴ ⚓ 🧺 🍺 ☕c 🔄 🚗 ⬇V ⊙

Humber Cruising Association Ltd

Meridan Quay
Auckland Road
Fish Docks, Grimsby
North East Lincolnshire
DN31 3RP
tel 01472 268424

Annual cost per metre:	£72.00
Overnight cost per metre:	£1.22
Number of berths:	170
Maximum length:	20
Tidal access:	HW±2

Facilities: ☺ WC ⬠ ☎ VHF 🛢D ⚓P ⊗P ⚓ 🧺 🚗 ⬇V

Tidemill Yacht Harbour Ltd

Woodbridge
Suffolk
IP12 1BP
tel 01394 385745

Annual cost per metre:	£143.06
Overnight cost per metre:	£1.40
Number of berths:	160
Maximum length:	20
Tidal access:	HW±3

Facilities: WC ⬠ ☎ VHF ⚓ 🛢D ⚓P ⚓N ⊗P ⊗N ⛴ ⚓ 🧺 🍺 ☕c ✂ 🔄 🚗 ⬇V ⊙ ♿

Debbage Yachting

The Quay
New Cut West
Ipswich
Suffolk
IP2 8HN
tel 01473 601169

Annual cost per metre:	£86.00
Overnight cost per metre:	£0.70
Number of berths:	50
Maximum length:	15
Tidal access:	HW±4.5

Facilities: WC 🛢D ⚓N ⊗P ⊗N ⛴ 🧺 🔄 🚗 ⬇V

1.5 Coastal - Scotland

Within this section marinas are listed in geographical order from Oban to Oban

Oban Yachts & Marine Services Ltd

Ardentrive
Kerrera
by Oban
Argyll
PA34 4SX
tel 01631 565333

Annual cost per metre:	£114.00
Overnight cost per metre:	£1.14
Number of berths:	35
Maximum length:	20
Tidal access:	All States

Facilities: 🚾 ⛽ 📞 VHF ⚓ ⛽ ♿ 🚻 ⚓ 🏠 🛒 📺 ⚓

Port Edgar Marina

Shore Road
South Queensferry
West Lothian
EH30 9SQ
tel 0131 3313330

Annual cost per metre:	£12.30
Overnight cost per metre:	£1.25
Number of berths:	320
Maximum length:	18
Tidal access:	All States

Facilities: 🚾 ⛽ 📞 VHF ⚓ ⛽ ♿ 🚻 ⚓ 🏠 🛒 🍴 ✂ 📺 🚗 ⚓ ♿

Peterhead Bay Marina

Bath House
Bath Street
Peterhead
Aberdeenshire
AB42 1DX
tel 01779 474020

Annual cost per metre:	£62.28
Overnight cost per metre:	£1.31
Number of berths:	160
Maximum length:	20
Tidal access:	All states

Facilities: 🚾 ⛽ 📞 ⚓ ⛽ ♿ 🚻 ⚓ 🚗 ⚓

Longman Yacht Haven

Inverness Harbour
Longman Drive
Inverness
IV1 1SU
tel 01463 715715

Annual cost per metre:	£55.55
Overnight cost per metre:	£1.11
Number of berths:	22
Maximum length:	12
Tidal access:	All states

Facilities: 🚾 📞 VHF ⚓ ♿ ! ⚓ 📺 ⚓

Melfort Pier & Harbour

The Pier
Kilmelford
By Oban
Argyll
PA34 4XD
tel 01852 200333

Annual cost per metre:	£c/m
Overnight cost per metre:	£0.88
Number of berths:	n/a
Maximum length:	180
Tidal access:	All states

Facilities: 🚾 ⛽ 📞 VHF ⛽ ♿ ⚓ ⚓ 🛒 🍴 🚗 ⚓ ⬜

Ardfern Yacht Centre

Ardfern
By Lochgilphead
Argyll
Scotland
PA31 8QN
tel 01852 500247

Annual cost per metre:	£193.00
Overnight cost per metre:	£1.30
Number of berths:	80
Maximum length:	25
Tidal access:	All states

Facilities: WC 🛒 ☎ VHF ⛽D ⚓P ⚓N ⊗P ⊗N ⚒ 🏗 🛒 🔌 🛒c 🔧 🚗 ⚓ 🛟v ⊙ ♿

Craobh Marina

Craobh Haven
By Lochgilphead
Argyll, Scotland
PA31 8UD
tel 01852 500222

Annual cost per metre:	£184.48
Overnight cost per metre:	£1.76
Number of berths:	250
Maximum length:	30
Tidal access:	All states

Facilities: ☺ WC 🛒 ☎ VHF ⛽D ⚓P ⊗P ⚒ 🏗 🛒 🔌 🛒c ✂ 🚗 🛟v ⊙

Tarbert Harbour

Harbour Masters' Office
Harbour Street
Tarbert
Argyll
PA29 6UD
tel 01880 820344

Annual cost per metre:	£93.73
Overnight cost per metre:	£1.18
Number of berths:	60
Maximum length:	14
Tidal access:	All states

Facilities: WC 🛒 ☎ VHF ⛽D ⛽P ⚓P ⚓N ⊗P ⊗N ⚓ 🛒 🛒c ✂ 🚗 🛟v ⊙ ♿

Rhu Marina Ltd

Rhu
Helensburgh
Dunbartonshire
G84 8LH
tel 01436 820238

Annual cost per metre:	£202.10
Overnight cost per metre:	£1.65
Number of berths:	190
Maximum length:	22
Tidal access:	All states

Facilities: WC 🛒 ☎ VHF ⚓ ⛽D ⚓P ⊗P 🏗 🛒 🛒c ✂ 🚗 🛟v

Kip Marina

Holt Leisure Parks Ltd
The Yacht Harbour
Inverkip
Renfrewshire
PA16 0AS
tel 01475 521485

Annual cost per metre:	£250.28
Overnight cost per metre:	£1.46
Number of berths:	700
Maximum length:	40
Tidal access:	All states

Facilities: WC 🛒 ☎ VHF ⚓ ⛽D ⛽P ⚓P ⊗P ⚒ 🏗 ⚓ 🛒 🔌 🛒c ✂ 🚗 ⚓ 🛟v ⊙

Largs Yacht Haven

Irvine Road
Largs
Ayrshire
KA30 8EZ
tel 01475 675333

Annual cost per metre:	£250.27
Overnight cost per metre:	£1.70
Number of berths:	630
Maximum length:	30
Tidal access:	All states

Facilities: ☺ WC ⌒ (VHF ⚲ ⛽D ⛽P ⚲P ⚲N ⊗P ⊗N ⚓ 工 ⚓ 🧺 🗋 ☕c ✂ 🔌 🚗 ⮣v ⊡ ♿

Troon Yacht Haven

The Harbour
Troon
Ayrshire
KA10 6DJ
tel 01292 315553

Annual cost per metre:	£190.35
Overnight cost per metre:	£1.53
Number of berths:	300
Maximum length:	37
Tidal access:	All states

Facilities: WC ⌒ (VHF ⚲ ⛽D ⚲P ⚲N ⊗P ⊗N ⚓ 工 ⚓ 🧺 🗋 ☕c ✂ 🔌 🚗 ⮣v ⊡

Dunstaffnage Marina

Dunbeg
by Oban
Argyll
Scotland
PA37 1PX
tel 01631 566555

Annual cost per metre:	£165.08
Overnight cost per metre:	£1.34
Number of berths:	65
Maximum length:	20
Tidal access:	All states

Facilities: WC ⌒ (VHF ⚲ ⛽D ⊗P ⚓ 工 🧺 🗋 ☕c ✂ 🔌 🚗 ⮣v

1.6 Coastal - North West

Within this section marinas are listed in geographical order from Lancaster to Maryport

Glasson Basin Yacht Co Ltd

Glasson Dock	
Lancaster	
Lancashire	
LA2 0AW	
tel 01524 751491	

Annual cost per metre:	£94.00
Overnight cost per metre:	£1.00
Number of berths:	250
Maximum length:	30
Tidal access:	HW±1

Facilities:

Fleetwood Harbour Village Marina

The Dock Office	
Wyre Dock	
Fleetwood	
Lancs	
FY7 6PP	
tel 01253 872323	

Annual cost per metre:	£123.00
Overnight cost per metre:	£1.50
Number of berths:	300
Maximum length:	20
Tidal access:	HW±1.5

Facilities:

Douglas Boatyard

Becconsall Lane	
Hesketh Bank	
Preston	
Lancashire	
PR4 6RR	
tel 01772 812462	

Annual cost per metre:	£70.00
Overnight cost per metre:	£c/m
Number of berths:	140
Maximum length:	30
Tidal access:	HW±2

Facilities:

Preston Marina

Navigation Way	
Riversway Docklands	
Preston	
Lancashire	
PR2 2YP	
tel 01772 733595	

Annual cost per metre:	£99.00
Overnight cost per metre:	£0.66
Number of berths:	125
Maximum length:	30
Tidal access:	HW-1+2

Facilities:

Liverpool Marina

Harbour Marina Plc	
Coburg Wharf	
Sefton Street	
Merseyside	
L3 4BP	
tel 0151 708 5228	

Annual cost per metre:	£135.71
Overnight cost per metre:	£1.35
Number of berths:	300
Maximum length:	28
Tidal access:	HW±2.5

Facilities:

Albert Dock

Royal Liver Building	Annual cost per metre: £c/m
Pier Head	Overnight cost per metre: £c/m
Liverpool	Number of berths: 18
Merseyside	Maximum length: 55
L3 1JH	Tidal access: HW±2
tel 0151 236 6090	

Facilities: [symbols]

Fiddlers Ferry Yacht Haven

Ferry Boat Yard	Annual cost per metre: £24.75
Penketh	Overnight cost per metre: £c/m
Warrington	Number of berths: 200
Cheshire	Maximum length: 20
WA5 2UJ	Tidal access: HW±1
tel 01925 727519	

Facilities: [symbols]

James Mayor & Co Ltd

Boat Yard	Annual cost per metre: £44.00
Tartleton	Overnight cost per metre: £c/m
Nr Preston	Number of berths: 80
Lancashire	Maximum length: 20
PR4 6HD	Tidal access: HW±2

Facilities: [symbols]

Maryport Marina

West Coast Sailing Ltd	Annual cost per metre: £117.50
Maryport Marina	Overnight cost per metre: £1.00
Maryport	Number of berths: 250
Cumbria	Maximum length: 30
CA15 8AD	Tidal access: HW±3
tel 01900 814431	

Facilities: [symbols]

Conwy Marina

Crest Nicholson Marinas Ltd	Annual cost per metre:	£199.75
Conwy Morfa	Overnight cost per metre:	£1.70
Conwy	Number of berths:	450
Gwynedd	Maximum length:	23.3
LL32 8EP	Tidal access:	HW±3
tel 01492 593000		

Facilities: ☺ 🚾 📷 📞 VHF ⚓ ⛽D ⛽P ✂P ⊙P ! 🏗 ⚓ 🍺 🛒c ✂ ▨ 🚗 🛟 ⊙

Port Dinorwic Marina

Yfelinneli	Annual cost per metre:	£204.14
Gwynedd	Overnight cost per metre:	£1.65
LL56 4JN	Number of berths:	200
tel 01248 671500	Maximum length:	30
	Tidal access:	HW±3

Facilities: ☺ 🚾 📷 📞 VHF ⚓ ⛽D ✂P ✂N ⊙P ⊙N ◤ 🏗 ⚓ 🍺 🍺 🛒c ✂ ▨ 🚗 🛟 ⊙ ♿

Hafan Pwllheli Marina

Glan Don	Annual cost per metre:	£199.75
Pwllheli	Overnight cost per metre:	£1.58
Gwynedd	Number of berths:	430
LL53 5YT	Maximum length:	25
tel 01758 701219	Tidal access:	All states

Facilities: ⊃ ☺ 🚾 📷 📞 VHF ⚓ ⛽D ⛽P ✂P ✂N ⊙P ⊙N ! ◤ 🏗 🍺 🛒c ✂ ▨ 🚗 🛟 ⊙ ♿

Milford Marina

The Docks		
Milford Haven	Annual cost per metre:	£115.00
Pembrokeshire	Overnight cost per metre:	£1.00
SA73 3AF	Number of berths:	250
tel 01646 696312	Maximum length:	80
	Tidal access:	HW±4

Facilities: 🚾 📷 📞 VHF ⚓ ⛽D ✂P ✂N ⊙P ◤ 🏗 🍺 🛒c ▨ 🚗 🛟 ⊙ ♿

Neyland Yacht Haven

Brunel Quay	Annual cost per metre:	£155.10
Neyland	Overnight cost per metre:	£1.18
Pembrokeshire	Number of berths:	360
SA73 1PY	Maximum length:	20
tel 01646 601601	Tidal access:	All states

Facilities: 🚾 📷 📞 VHF ⚓ ⛽D ✂P ✂N ⊙P ⊙N ◤ 🏗 🍺 🛒c ✂ ▨ 🚗 🛟 ⊙ ♿

Aberystwyth Marina

Y Lanfa - Aberystwyth Marina	Annual cost per metre:	£130.00
Trefechan	Overnight cost per metre:	£1.30
Aberystwyth	Number of berths:	101
Ceredigion	Maximum length:	20
SY23 1AS	Tidal access:	HW±3
tel 01970 611422		

Facilities: [icons]

Swansea Marina

Lockside	Annual cost per metre:	£139.00
Maritime Quarter	Overnight cost per metre:	£1.11
Swansea	Number of berths:	356
Glamorgan	Maximum length:	n/a
tel 01792 470310	Tidal access:	HW±4

Facilities: [icons]

Penarth Marina

Crest Nicholson Marinas	Annual cost per metre:	£165.00
Portway Village	Overnight cost per metre:	£1.60
Penarth	Number of berths:	350
Vale of Glamorgan	Maximum length:	30
CF64 1TQ	Tidal access:	HW±3.75
tel 01222 705021		

Facilities: [icons]

Within this section marinas are listed in geographical order from Coleraine to Coleraine

Coleraine Marina

64 Portstewart Rd
Coleraine
Co. Londonderry
N Ireland
BT55 1RS
tel 01265 44768

Annual cost per metre:	£48.00
Overnight cost per metre:	£c/m
Number of berths:	55
Maximum length:	20
Tidal access:	All states

Facilities: ☺ 🅆 ℘ ☏ VHF ⚓ 🛢D 🛢P ⚡P ⚡N ⊗P ⊗N ! ⚓ 🏗 🛒 🍺 🛒c 🔧 🚗 ⬇v

Bangor Marina

Bregenz House
Quay Street
Bangor
Co Down
BT20 5ED
tel 01247 453297

Annual cost per metre:	£157.50
Overnight cost per metre:	£1.50
Number of berths:	550
Maximum length:	80
Tidal access:	All states

Facilities: 🅆 ℘ ☏ VHF ⚓ 🛢D 🛢P ⚡P ⚡N ⊗P ⊗N ⚓ 🏗 🛒 🍺 🛒c 🔧 🚗 ⬇v ▣ ♿

Carrickfergus Marina

Rodger's Quay
Carrickfergus
Co Antrim
Northern Ireland
BT38 8BE
tel 01960 366666

Annual cost per metre:	£125.97
Overnight cost per metre:	£1.50
Number of berths:	300
Maximum length:	25
Tidal access:	c/m

Facilities: ☺ 🅆 ℘ ☏ VHF ⚓ 🛢D ⚡P ⊗P ⚓ 🏗 🛒 🍺 🚗 ⬇v ▣

Seatons Marina

8 Drumslade Road
Coleraine
Co Londonderry
Northern Ireland
BT52 1SE
tel 01265 832086

Annual cost per metre:	£60.00
Overnight cost per metre:	£1.00
Number of berths:	70
Maximum length:	15
Tidal access:	All states

Facilities: VHF ⚓ 🛢D ⚡N ⊗N ⚓ 🏗 ⚓ 🛒c 🚗 ⬇v

1.9 Coastal - Channel Islands

Within this section marinas are listed in geographical order from St Peter Port to St Helier

St Peter Port Marinas

Harbour Office
St Julians's Emplacement
St Peter Port
Guernsey
GY1 1LW
tel 01481 725987

Annual cost per metre:	£n/a
Overnight cost per metre:	£1.40
Number of berths:	1650
Maximum length:	20
Tidal access:	HW±2.5

Facilities: WC 🏠 ☎ VHF ⚓ ⛽D ⛽P ⚡P ⚡N 🔌P 🔌N ⚓ ⚓ 🛒 🍴 🧺c ✂ 🔲 ⚓ 💿 ♿

Elizabeth Marina

La Route Du Port Elizabeth
St Helier
Jersey
Channel Islands
tel 01534 885588

Annual cost per metre:	£184.68
Overnight cost per metre:	£n/a
Number of berths:	575
Maximum length:	20
Tidal access:	HW±3

Facilities: WC 🏠 ☎ ⛽D ⛽P ⚡P 🔌P ! ⚓ 🧺 🚗

La Collette Yacht Basin

La Collette
St Helier
Jersey
Channel Islands
tel 01534 885529

Annual cost per metre:	£198.50
Overnight cost per metre:	£1.44
Number of berths:	100
Maximum length:	17
Tidal access:	All states

Facilities: ☺ WC 🏠 ☎ ⚡P 🔌P ⚓ ⚓ ⚓ 🧺 🚗 ⚓ ♿

Victoria Marina

Harbour Office
St Julian's Emplacement
St Peter Port
Guernsey
GY1 2LW
tel 01481 725987

Annual cost per metre:	£82.20
Overnight cost per metre:	£1.54
Number of berths:	1800
Maximum length:	14
Tidal access:	HW±2.5

Facilities: WC 🏠 ☎ VHF ⚓ ⛽D ⛽P ⚡P 🔌P ⚓ ⚓ 🛒 🍴 🧺c ✂ 🔲 ⚓ 💿

St Helier Marina

New North Quay
St Helier
Jersey
Channel Islands
JE4 9XF
tel 01534 885508

Annual cost per metre:	£192.07
Overnight cost per metre:	£1.44
Number of berths:	120
Maximum length:	17
Tidal access:	HW±3

Facilities: ☺ WC 🏠 ☎ ⚓ ⚡P 🔌P ! ⚓ 🧺 🚗 ⚓ 💿

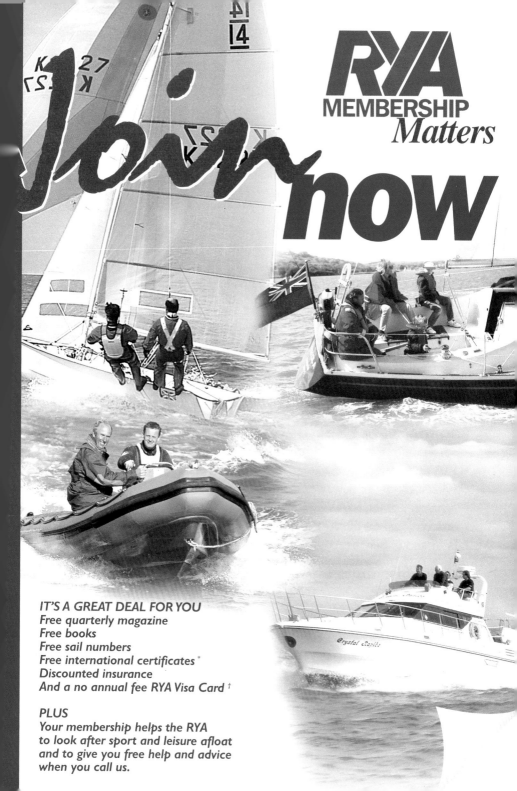

Join now

RYA MEMBERSHIP *Matters*

IT'S A GREAT DEAL FOR YOU
Free quarterly magazine
Free books
Free sail numbers
Free international certificates *
Discounted insurance
And a no annual fee RYA Visa Card †

PLUS
Your membership helps the RYA
to look after sport and leisure afloat
and to give you free help and advice
when you call us.

RYA MEMBERSHIP *Matters*

It's a great deal for you...

Membership costs very little...
- Personal Membership £25 (or £23 by direct debit)
- Under 21 £10
- Family Membership £40 (or £38 by direct debit)

and there are FREE BENEFITS...
- Four editions of RYA Magazine every year
- RYA publications
- Allocation of sail numbers
- A no annual fee RYA Visa Card†
- International certificates of competence *
- Boat show lounges

special discounts on
- Boat insurance

...and more
As an RYA member you can talk directly to us and get information and legal advice on all aspects of leisure boating from inland waters cruising to Olympic racing.

You can benefit from all this expertise by joining now... then simply pick up the phone the next time you need advice.

†Only available to UK residents aged 18 years and over and subject to status.   *If you qualify

and important for sport and leisure afloat

So, those are the benefits, but what happens to your subscription?

Your subscriptions enable us to work for the interests, and protect the freedoms of, *everyone* who enjoys boating.

Imagine a world where the RYA did not work with UK and EU legislators to protect your freedom to cruise the inland waterways, estuaries and seaways as you always have. Suppose there was nobody setting minimum safety standards and providing high quality training schemes for schools and instructors. Imagine no one working to attract people into the sport, or developing the potential of talented young sailors and powerboat racers. Imagine not having a strong team to represent us at the Olympic Games, or a collective voice to improve cruising facilities and marina standards.

It's the RYA that does all these things, and more – and it's your membership that makes it happen.

please join now

Your membership matters. It's important for everyone who enjoys their sport and leisure afloat - and it's a great deal for you.
There is a membership form overleaf for you to use

Yes I want to join the RYA

Type of Membership Required: (tick as applicable)

☐ **Personal £25** (*£23* if you pay by Direct Debit)

☐ **Family £40** (*£38* if you pay by Direct Debit)

☐ **Under 21 £10**

Please indicate your main boating interest by ticking one box only

W	SC	SR	PR	MC	PW

W=Windsurfing   SC=Sail Cruising
SR=Sail Racing   PR=Powerboat Racing
MC=Motor Cruising   PW=Personal Watercraft

	Title	Forename	Surname	Date of Birth	Male
1.					
2.					
3.					
4.					

Address

Town   County   Postcode

Signature --

THE EASY WAY TO PAY

INSTRUCTIONS TO YOUR BANK OR BUILDING SOCIETY TO PAY DIRECT DEBITS

Originators identification number

9	5	5	2	1	3

DIRECT Debit

Please complete this form and return it to:
Royal Yachting Association RYA House Romsey Road Eastleigh Hampshire SO50 9YA. Tel: 01703 627400

To The Manager _____

_____ **Bank or Building Society**

Address _____

_____ **Post Code** _____

2. Name(s) of account holder(s)

3. Branch Sort Code

| | | — | | | — | | |

4. Bank or Building Society account number

5. RYA Membership Number (For office use only)

6. Instruction to pay your Bank or Building Society

Please pay Royal Yachting Association Direct Debits from the account detailed on this instruction subject to the safeguards assured by The Direct Debit Guarantee

Signature(s) _____

Date _____

Cash, Cheque, Postal Order enclosed £ [   ] Made payable to the Royal Yachting Association

077

Office use only: Membership No. Allocated

Office use / Centre Stamp

Beaucette Marina

Vale
Guernsey
Channel Islands
GY3 5BQ
tel 01481 45000

Annual cost per metre: £249.00
Overnight cost per metre: £1.95
Number of berths: 140
Maximum length: 25
Tidal access: HW±3.5

Facilities: 🚾 📷 ☎ VHF ⛽ᴅ ⚡ᴘ ⚡ɴ 🅿ᴘ 🅿ɴ 🛥 🏗 ⚓ 🧺 🛢 🚗 ⬇ᵛ ⊙

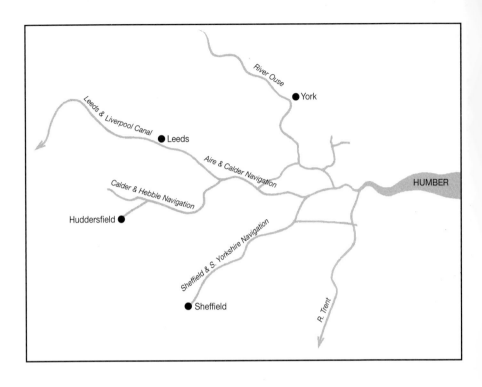

Aire & Calder Navigation
Stanley Ferry Marina

Ferry Lane	Annual cost per metre:	£c/m
Stanley Ferry	Overnight cost per metre:	£c/m
Wakefield	Number of berths:	200
W Yorks	Maximum length:	c/m
WF3 4LT	Tidal access:	Non tidal
tel 01924 201117		

Facilities: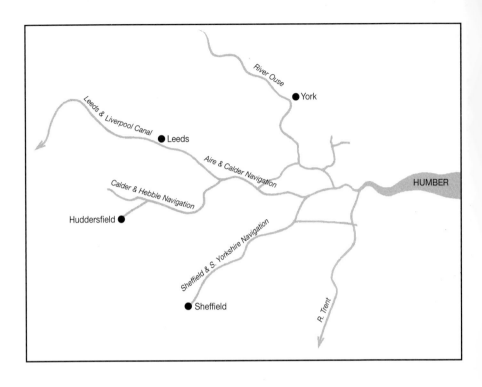

Bridgewater Canal
Lymm Marina

Warrington Lane	Annual cost per metre:	£c/m
Lymm	Overnight cost per metre:	£c/m
Cheshire	Number of berths:	30
WA13 0SW	Maximum length:	n/a
tel 01925 752945	Tidal access:	Non tidal

Facilities: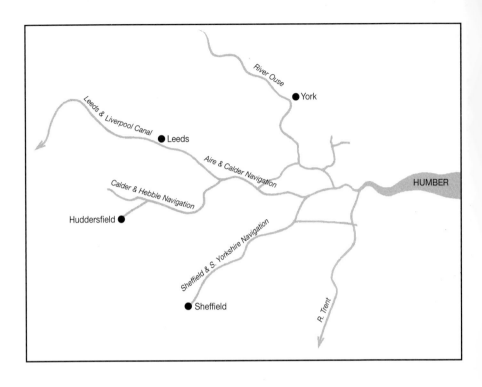

Bridgewater Canal
Preston Brook Marina

Marina House	Annual cost per metre:	£c/m
Preston Brook Marina	Overnight cost per metre:	£c/m
Runcorn	Number of berths:	300
Cheshire	Maximum length:	n/a
WA7 3AF	Tidal access:	Non tidal
tel 01928 719081		

Facilities: 🚾 ⛽ ✂ ⊗ₙ ⚓ 🧺 🚗

Calder & Hebble Navigation/Rochdale Canal
Sowerby Bridge Canal Basin

Shire Cruisers	Annual cost per metre:	£c/m
The Wharf	Overnight cost per metre:	£c/m
Sowerby Bridge	Number of berths:	60
West Yorkshire	Maximum length:	18
HX6 2AG	Tidal access:	Non tidal
tel 01422 832712		

Facilities: 🚾 ⛽ᴅ ⚙ₚ ⚙ₙ ⊗ₙ ! ⚓ 🏗 ⊥ 🛒 🛢 🛒c 🚲 🚗 ⬇

Huddersfield Broad Canal
Aspley Wharf Marina Ltd

Aspley Basin	Annual cost per metre:	£60.00
Huddersfield	Overnight cost per metre:	£1.50
West Yorkshire	Number of berths:	10
HD1 6SD	Maximum length:	20
tel 01484 514123	Tidal access:	Non tidal

Facilities: 🚾 ⛽ ⊗ₙ ⚓ 🛒 🛢 🛒c 🚲 ⬇

Lake Windermere
Windermere Marina Village

Nabwood	Annual cost per metre:	£c/m
Bowness-on-Windermere	Overnight cost per metre:	£c/m
Cumbria	Number of berths:	430
LA23 3JQ	Maximum length:	15
tel 01539 446551	Tidal access:	Non tidal

Facilities: 🚾 ⛽ 📞 ✂ ⛽ᴅ ⚙ₙ ⊗ₚ ⊗ₙ ⚓ 🏗 🛒 🛢 🛒c 🚲 🚗 ⬇ 🔲

Leeds & Liverpool Canal
White Bear Marina

Park Road	Annual cost per metre:	£80.26
Adlington	Overnight cost per metre:	£0.56
Nr Chorley	Number of berths:	140
Lancashire	Maximum length:	18.8
PR7 4HZ	Tidal access:	All states
tel 01257 481054		

Facilities: 🚾 ⛽ 📞 ✂ ⛽ᴅ ⚙ₚ ⚙ₙ ⊗ₚ ⊗ₙ ! ⚓ 🏗 ⊥ 🛒 🛢 🛒c 🚲 🚗 ⬇ 🔲

River Ouse
Naburn Marina Ltd

Naburn	Annual cost per metre:	£95.00
York	Overnight cost per metre:	£0.55
North Yorkshire	Number of berths:	500
YO1 4RW	Maximum length:	15
tel 01904 621021	Tidal access:	n/a

Facilities: [WC] 🏴 📞 VHF ⚓ ⛽D ⛽P ⚡P ⊗P ! ⚓ 🏗 ⚓ 🫖 🧺c 🅿 🚗 ⬇v

River Trent
Colwick Park Marina

River Road	Annual cost per metre:	£76.00
Off Mile End Road	Overnight cost per metre:	£0.67
Colwick	Number of berths:	224
Nottinghamshire	Maximum length:	50
NG4 2DW	Tidal access:	n/a
tel 0115 987 0785		

Facilities: [WC] 📞 ⚓ ⊗N ! ⚓ 🧺 🫖 🚗 ⬇v ⓞ

River Trent
Farndon Marina

North End	Annual cost per metre:	£81.43
Farndon	Overnight cost per metre:	£0.55
Newark-on-Trent	Number of berths:	326
Nottinghamshire	Maximum length:	38
NG24 3SX	Tidal access:	n/a
tel 01636 705483		

Facilities: [WC] 🏴 📞 VHF ⚓ ⛽D ⚡P ⚡N ⊗P ⊗N ! ⚓ 🏗 🧺 🫖 🧺c 🅿 🚗 ⬇v ⓞ

River Trent
Newark Marina

26 Farndon Road	Annual cost per metre:	£88.60
Newark	Overnight cost per metre:	£0.55
Nottinghamshire	Number of berths:	120
NG24 4SD	Maximum length:	14
tel 01636 704022	Tidal access:	Non tidal

Facilities: [WC] 🏴 ⚓ ⛽D ⚡P ⊗P 🏗 ⚓ 🧺 🧺c 🅿 🚗 ⬇v

River Trent
Sawley Marina Ltd

Sawley	Annual cost per metre:	£69.03
Long Eaton	Overnight cost per metre:	£0.58
Nottingham	Number of berths:	370
NG10 3AE	Maximum length:	24.4
tel 0115 973 4278	Tidal access:	Non tidal

Facilities: [WC] 🏴 📞 ⛽D ⛽P ⚡P ⚡N ⊗P ⊗N ! ⚓ 🏗 ⚓ 🧺 🫖 🧺c 🅿 🚗 ⬇v ⓞ ♿

River Trent
Shardlow Marina

London Road
Shardlow
Derby
Derbys
DE72 2GL
tel 01332 792832

Annual cost per metre:	£55.35
Overnight cost per metre:	£0.50
Number of berths:	300
Maximum length:	23.3
Tidal access:	All states

Facilities: ᵂᶜ 🏮 🅿D 🚿P ⓦP ! ⛵ ⚓ 🧺 🪣 🚽c 🖼 🚗 ⛴

River Tyne
St Peters Marina

St Peters Basin
Newcastle-upon-Tyne
Tyne & Wear
NE6 1HX
tel 0191 265 4472

Annual cost per metre:	£136.30
Overnight cost per metre:	£1.17
Number of berths:	130
Maximum length:	37
Tidal access:	HW±4

Facilities: ᵂᶜ 🏮 ☎ VHF 🛠 🅿D 🅿P ⓦP ⓦN 🚿P 🚿N ! ⛵ 🏗 ⚓ 🧺 🪣 🚽c ✂ 🖼 🚗 ⛴ ⊡

River Ure
Boroughbridge Marina

Roe Cliffe Lane
Boroughbridge
North Yorkshire
YO5 9LJ
tel 01904 728229

Annual cost per metre:	£108.10
Overnight cost per metre:	£n/a
Number of berths:	80
Maximum length:	17
Tidal access:	Non tidal

Facilities: ᵂᶜ 🛠 🚿P 🚿P ⛵ ⚓ 🧺 🪣 🚗

Stainforth-Keadby Canal
Blue Water Marina

South End
Thorne
Doncaster
South Yorkshire
DN8 5QR
tel 01405 813165

Annual cost per metre:	£60.08
Overnight cost per metre:	£0.22
Number of berths:	120
Maximum length:	25
Tidal access:	Non tidal

Facilities: ᵂᶜ 🏮 🛠 🅿D ⓦN 🚿N ! ⛵ 🏗 🪣 🚽c 🖼 🚗 ⛴

Trent
Staniland of Thorne Marina Ltd

Lock Lane
Thorne
Doncaster
South Yorkshire
DN8 5ES
tel 01405 813150

Annual cost per metre:	£80.65
Overnight cost per metre:	£0.00
Number of berths:	90
Maximum length:	25+
Tidal access:	All states

Facilities: ᵂᶜ 🏮 ☎ 🛠 🅿D 🚿P ⓦN 🚿P 🚿N ! ⛵ 🏗 🪣 🚽c 🖼 🚗 ⛴

Upper Peak Forest Canal
New Mills Wharf

Hibbert Street	Annual cost per metre:	£c/m
New Mills	Overnight cost per metre:	£c/m
Stockport	Number of berths:	40
Cheshire	Maximum length:	n/a
SK12 3JJ	Tidal access:	n/a
tel 01663 745000		

Facilities: [symbols]

Windermere
Windermere Aquatic Ltd

Glebe Rd	Annual cost per metre:	£c/m
Bowness-on-Windermere	Overnight cost per metre:	£c/m
Cumbria	Number of berths:	n/a
tel 01966 22121	Maximum length:	15
	Tidal access:	Non tidal

Facilities: [symbols]

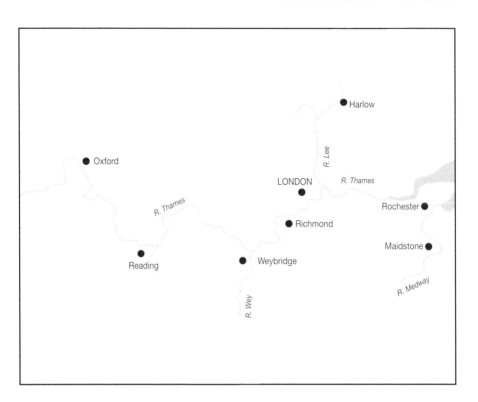

Kennet & Avon Canal
Froud's Bridge Marina

Froud's Lane	Annual cost per metre:	£99.98
Aldermarston	Overnight cost per metre:	£0.45
Berkshire	Number of berths:	100
RG7 4LH	Maximum length:	22
tel 0118 971 4508	Tidal access:	n/a

Facilities: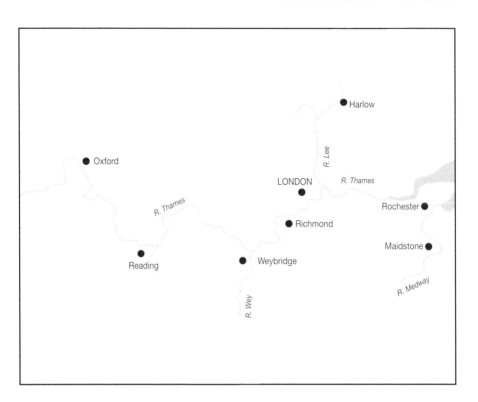

Kentish Stour
Highway Marine Ltd

Pillory Gate Wharf	Annual cost per metre:	£80.56
Strand Street	Overnight cost per metre:	£1.60
Sandwich	Number of berths:	60
Kent	Maximum length:	15
CT13 9EU	Tidal access:	HW±2
tel 01304 613925		

Facilities:

Oxford Canal
Napton Marina

Tomlow Road	Annual cost per metre:	£c/m
Stockton	Overnight cost per metre:	£c/m
Rugby	Number of berths:	70
Warwickshire	Maximum length:	n/a
CV23 8HX	Tidal access:	Non tidal
tel 01926 813644		

Facilities: ᵂᶜ ⌀ 🅿ᴅ 🅿ᴘ ✎ᴘ ⊗ᴘ ! 🛒c 🔁 🚗

River Arun
Ship & Anchor Marina

Ford	Annual cost per metre:	£139.00
Arundel	Overnight cost per metre:	£n/a
West Sussex	Number of berths:	32
BN18 OBJ	Maximum length:	11
tel 01243 551262	Tidal access:	All states

Facilities: ᵂᶜ ⌐ ☎ ⊗ᴘ ⟰ 🛒 📙 🔁 🚗

River Avon (Avon)
Bristol Marina

Hanover Place	Annual cost per metre:	£139.00
Bristol	Overnight cost per metre:	£1.00
Avon	Number of berths:	n/a
BS1 6TZ	Maximum length:	20
tel 0117 921 3198	Tidal access:	HW±3

Facilities: ᵂᶜ ⌐ ☎ VHF ⌀ 🅿ᴅ ✎ᴘ ✎ᴺ ⊗ᴘ ! ⟰ ⟟ ⟱ 🛒 🛒c ✂ 🔁 🚗 Lⱽ ▢

River Crouch
Essex Marina

Wallasea Island	Annual cost per metre:	£175.41
Near Rochford	Overnight cost per metre:	£c/m
Essex	Number of berths:	380
SS4 2HF	Maximum length:	30
tel 01702 258531	Tidal access:	All states

Facilities: ᵂᶜ ⌐ ☎ VHF ⌀ 🅿ᴅ 🅿ᴘ ✎ᴘ ⊗ᴘ ⟰ ⟟ ⟱ 🛒 📙 🛒c 🔁 🚗 Lⱽ ▢

River Dart
Dolphin Haven

Dolphin Shipyard	Annual cost per metre:	£185.79
Galmpton	Overnight cost per metre:	£0.78
Nr Brixham	Number of berths:	32
Devon	Maximum length:	11
TQ5 0EH	Tidal access:	HW±2
tel 01803 842424		

Facilities: ᵂᶜ ⌐ ⌀ 🅿ᴅ ✎ᴺ ⊗ᴘ ⊗ᴺ ⟟ ⟱ 🛒c 🔁 🚗 Lⱽ

River Dart
Hole Farm Moorings

Hole Farm
Dittisham
Dartmouth
Devon
TQ6 0JG
tel 01803 722340

Annual cost per metre:	£n/a
Overnight cost per metre:	£1.00
Number of berths:	55
Maximum length:	12
Tidal access:	HW ±4

Facilities: ⚓ 🧺 🚗

River Itchen
Kemps Quay

Quayside Road
Bitterne Manor
Southampton
Hampshire
SO18 1BZ
tel 01703 632323

Annual cost per metre:	£c/m
Overnight cost per metre:	£1.96
Number of berths:	180
Maximum length:	15
Tidal access:	c/m

Facilities: 🅆 ☂ 📞 ⛽P ⛽N ⊛P 🏗 ⚓ 🧺 🧺c 🚗 ⚓v

River Lee
Lee Valley Marina (Stanstead Abbott)

South Street
Stanstead Abbotts
Ware
Herts
SG12 8AL
tel 01920 870499

Annual cost per metre:	£124.85
Overnight cost per metre:	£0.34
Number of berths:	100
Maximum length:	28
Tidal access:	n/a

Facilities: 🅆 ☂ 📞 ⛽D ⛽N ⊛N ! ⛵ 🏗 ⚓ 🧺 🔁 🚗 ⚓v

River Lee
Lee Valley Marina - Springfield

Spring Hill
London
E5 9BL
tel 0181 806 1717

Annual cost per metre:	£138.24
Overnight cost per metre:	£1.15
Number of berths:	190
Maximum length:	22
Tidal access:	n/a

Facilities: 🅆 ☂ 📞 ✂ ⛽D ⛽P ⛽N ⊛P ⊛N ! ⛵ 🏗 🧺 🔌 🔁 ⚓v

River Medway
Allington Marina

Castle Road
Allington
Maidstone
Kent
ME16 0NH
tel 01622 752057

Annual cost per metre:	£125.56
Overnight cost per metre:	£0.84
Number of berths:	90
Maximum length:	15
Tidal access:	HW±2

Facilities: 🅆 ☂ 📞 ✂ ⛽D ⛽P ⛽P ⛽N ⊛P ⊛N ⛵ 🏗 ⚓ 🧺 🧺c 🔁 🚗 ⚓v

River Medway
Elmhaven Marina

The Boathouse, Rochester Road	Annual cost per metre:	£11.48
Halling	Overnight cost per metre:	£0.62
Rochester	Number of berths:	40
Kent	Maximum length:	35
ME2 1AQ	Tidal access:	All states
tel 01634 240489		

Facilities: ⌷ ⌷ ⌷ ⌷ₚ ⌷ₙ ⌷ₚ ⌷ₙ ⌷ ⌷ ⌷ ⌷ ⌷ ⌷

River Medway
Port Medway Marina

Station Road	Annual cost per metre:	£140.10
Cuxton	Overnight cost per metre:	£10.00
Rochester	Number of berths:	150
Kent	Maximum length:	30
ME2 1AB	Tidal access:	All states
tel 01634 720033		

Facilities: ☺ ⌷ ⌷ ⌷ VHF ⌷ ⌷ᴅ ⌷ₚ ⌷ₙ ⌷ₚ ⌷ₙ ! ⌷ ⌷ ⌷ ⌷ ⌷ ⌷ᴄ ⌷ ⌷

River Medway
Twyford Bridge Marina

Hampstead Lane	Annual cost per metre:	£c/m
Yalding	Overnight cost per metre:	£c/m
Kent	Number of berths:	80
ME18 6HG	Maximum length:	c/m
tel 01622 814378	Tidal access:	HW±3

Facilities: ⌷ ⌷ ⌷ᴅ ⌷ₙ ⌷ₙ ! ⌷ ⌷ ⌷ ⌷

River Thames
Bates Marina

W Bates & Son Boatbuilders Ltd	Annual cost per metre:	£170.00
Bridge Wharf	Overnight cost per metre:	£1.50
Chertsey	Number of berths:	115
Surrey	Maximum length:	13.7
KT16 8LG	Tidal access:	Non tidal
tel 01932 562255		

Facilities: ⌷ ⌷ ⌷ₚ ⌷ₙ ⌷ₚ ⌷ₙ ⌷ ⌷ ⌷ ⌷ᴄ ⌷ ⌷ ⌷

River Thames
Bossoms Boatyard

Binsey Village	Annual cost per metre:	£87.58
Oxford	Overnight cost per metre:	£1.29
Oxon	Number of berths:	115
OX2 0NL	Maximum length:	18
tel 01865 247780	Tidal access:	Non tidal

Facilities: ⌷ₙ ⌷ₙ ⌷ ⌷ᴄ ⌷ ⌷ ⌷

River Thames
Bourne End Marina

Wharf Lane	Annual cost per metre:	£162.00
Bourne End	Overnight cost per metre:	£0.45
Buckinghamshire	Number of berths:	130
SL8 5RR	Maximum length:	11
tel 01628 522813	Tidal access:	All states

Facilities: ᵂᶜ ⌀ 🅟ᴅ ⚡ₙ ⊗ₙ ! 🎏 ⚓ 🧺 ✂ 🔌 🚗 ⬇ᵛ

River Thames
Bray Marina

Monkey Island Lane	Annual cost per metre:	£193.00
Bray	Overnight cost per metre:	£1.31
Maidenhead	Number of berths:	400
Berkshire	Maximum length:	19
SL6 2EB	Tidal access:	All states
tel 01628 623654		

Facilities: ᵂᶜ 🛈 ☎ ⌀ 🅟ᴅ 🅟ᴾ ⚡ᴾ ⚡ₙ ⊗ᴾ ⊗ₙ 🎏 ⚓ 🧺 🔌 🔌c 🔌 🚗 ⬇ᵛ ♿

River Thames
Brentford Dock Marina

2 Justin Close	Annual cost per metre:	£132.19
Brentford Dock	Overnight cost per metre:	£c/m
Brentford	Number of berths:	60
Middlesex	Maximum length:	25
TW8 8QE	Tidal access:	HW±2.5
tel 0181 568 5096		

Facilities: ☺ ᵂᶜ 🛈 ☎ ⌀ ⚡ᴾ ⊗ᴾ ⊗ₙ 🧺 🔌 ⬇ᵛ ♿

River Thames
Cadogan Pier

Cheyne Walk	Annual cost per metre:	£177.38
Chelsea	Overnight cost per metre:	£3.91
Nr Albert Bridge	Number of berths:	30
London	Tidal access:	All states
SW3 5QR		
tel 0171 351 0927		

Facilities: ᵂᶜ ⌀ ⚡ᴾ ⊗ᴾ ! ⬇ᵛ

River Thames
Chelsea Harbour

Chelsea Harbour Ltd	Annual cost per metre:	£197.40
107-108 The Chambers	Overnight cost per metre:	£12.50
London	Number of berths:	55
SW10 0XF	Maximum length:	24
tel 0171 351 4433	Tidal access:	HW±1.5

Facilities: ᵂᶜ 🛈 ☎ VHF ⌀ ⚡ᴾ ⚡ₙ ⊗ᴾ ! 🔌 🚗 ⬇ᵛ

River Thames
Chiswick Quay Marina

Marina Office	Annual cost per metre: £139.12
Chiswick Quay	Overnight cost per metre: £c/m
London	Number of berths: 56
W4 3UR	Maximum length: 16
tel 0181 994 8743	Tidal access: HW±2

Facilities: ᵂᶜ 👜 VHF ⚓ ⚡ₚ ⊗ₙ 🛟 🧺 🔲 🚗 Ⓛᵥ

River Thames
Hambleden Mill Marina

Mill End	Annual cost per metre: £205.56
Henley-on-Thames	Overnight cost per metre: £n/a
Oxon	Number of berths: 80
RG9 3AY	Maximum length: 10
tel 01491 571316	Tidal access: Non tidal

Facilities: ᵂᶜ 👜 ⚓ ⚡ₚ ⚡ₙ ⊗ₙ 🏗 ⚓ 🔲 🚗

River Thames
Harleyford Estate Ltd

Henley Road	Annual cost per metre: £170.38
Marlow	Overnight cost per metre: £1.60
Bucks	Number of berths: 325
SL7 2DX	Maximum length: 16
tel 01628 471361	Tidal access: All states

Facilities: ᵂᶜ 👜 📞 ⚓ ⚡ₚ ⊗ₚ 🛟 🏗 ⚓ 🧺 🅿 🛢ᶜ 🔲 🚗 Ⓛᵥ ⊙

River Thames
Penton Hook Marina

Staines Road	Annual cost per metre: £198.00
Chertsey	Overnight cost per metre: £1.33
Surrey	Number of berths: 610
KT16 8PY	Maximum length: c/m
tel 01932 568468	Tidal access: All states

Facilities: ☺ ᵂᶜ 👜 📞 VHF ⚓ ⛽ᴅ ⛽ₚ ⚡ₚ ⚡ₙ ⊗ₚ ! 🏗 ⚓ 🧺 🅿 🛢ᶜ 🔲 🚗 Ⓛᵥ ♿

River Thames
Racecourse Yacht Basin

Maidenhead Road	Annual cost per metre: £200.00
Windsor	Overnight cost per metre: £1.11
Berkshire	Number of berths: 200
SL4 5HT	Maximum length: 13.5
tel 01753 851501	Tidal access: n/a

Facilities: ᵂᶜ 👜 📞 ⚓ ⛽ᴅ ⛽ₚ ⚡ₙ ⊗ₚ 🛟 🏗 ⚓ 🧺 🅿 🛢ᶜ 🔲 🚗 Ⓛᵥ

River Thames
Riverside Lechlade Marina

Park End Wharf	Annual cost per metre:	£69.89
Lechlade	Overnight cost per metre:	£1.10
Gloucestershire	Number of berths:	100
GL7 3AQ	Maximum length:	25
tel 01367 252229	Tidal access:	Non tidal

Facilities: 🆆 ⌂ ☎ ⚲ 🛢D 🛢P ⚡P ⚡N ⊛P ⊛N ⚓ 🏗 ⎁ ⛟ 🛒 🗏 🛒c ✂ 🔧 🚗 📶 💿 ♿

River Thames
Shepperton Marina Ltd

Felix Lane	Annual cost per metre:	£182.00
Shepperton	Overnight cost per metre:	£c/m
Middlesex	Number of berths:	270
TW17 8NS	Maximum length:	20
tel 01932 243722	Tidal access:	Non tidal

Facilities: 🆆 ⌂ ☎ VHF ⚲ 🛢D 🛢P ⚡P ⚡N ⊛P ⊛N ! 🏗 ⎁ 🛒 🛒c 🔧 🚗 📶

River Thames
South Dock Marina

Rope Street	Annual cost per metre:	£146.87
Plough Way	Overnight cost per metre:	£1.33
London	Number of berths:	250
SE16 1TX	Maximum length:	32
tel 0171 252 2244	Tidal access:	HW±2

Facilities: ☺ 🆆 ⌂ ☎ VHF ⚡P ⊛P ! ⚓ 🏗 ⎁ 🛒 🗏 ✂ 🔧 🚗 📶 ♿

River Thames
Temple Marina

Unit 25, Bourne End Mills	Annual cost per metre:	£182.00
Bourne End Lane	Overnight cost per metre:	£n/a
Hemel Hempstead	Number of berths:	65
Hertfordshire	Maximum length:	15.5
HP1 2RW	Tidal access:	Non tidal
tel 01442 862850		

Facilities: 🆆 ⌂ ☎ 🛢D ⚡P ⊛P ⎁ 🚗

River Thames
Thames & Kennet Marina

Caversham Lakes	Annual cost per metre:	£220.00
Henley Road	Overnight cost per metre:	£c/m
Reading	Number of berths:	280
Berkshire	Maximum length:	n/a
RG4 6LQ	Tidal access:	c/m
tel 0118 948 2911		

Facilities: 🆆 ⌂ ☎ ⚲ 🛢D ⚡P ⚡N ⊛P ⊛N ! 🏗 ⎁ 🛒 🛒c ✂ 🔧 🚗 📶

River Thames
Thames (Ditton) Marina

Portsmouth Road	Annual cost per metre:	£191.41
Surbiton	Overnight cost per metre:	£0.83
Surrey	Number of berths:	130
KT6 5QD	Maximum length:	14
tel 0181 398 6159	Tidal access:	Non tidal

Facilities: [WC] 🚰 ⚓ ! ⚓ 🏗 ⚓ 🛒 🛒c 🅿 🚗 ⚓

River Thames
Val Wyatt Marine - Willow Marina

Willow Lane	Annual cost per metre:	£228.00
Wargrave On Thames	Overnight cost per metre:	£c/m
Berkshire	Number of berths:	120
RG10 8LH	Maximum length:	18.3
tel 0118 940 3211	Tidal access:	Non tidal

Facilities: [WC] ⚓ ⚓ ⚓ 🚰 🚰 ⚓ ⚓ ⚓ ⚓ 🏗 ⚓ 🛒 🛒c ✂ 🅿 🚗 ⚓

River Thames
Walton Marina

Walton Bridge	Annual cost per metre:	£207.75
Walton-on-Thames	Overnight cost per metre:	£1.65
Surrey	Number of berths:	200
KT12 1QW	Maximum length:	20
tel 01932 226266	Tidal access:	Non tidal

Facilities: [WC] ⚓ ⚓ ⚓ ⚓ ⚓ ! ⚓ 🏗 ⚓ 🛒 📙 🛒c 🅿 🚗 ⚓

River Thames
Windsor Marina

Maidenhead Road	Annual cost per metre:	£218.00
Windsor	Overnight cost per metre:	£c/m
Berkshire	Number of berths:	200
SL4 5TZ	Maximum length:	15
tel 01753 853911	Tidal access:	All states

Facilities: [WC] ⚓ ⚓ ⚓ ⚓ ⚓ ⚓ ⚓ ! ⚓ 🏗 ⚓ 🛒 🅿 🚗 ⚓

River Waveney
Burgh Castle Marina

Butt Lane	Annual cost per metre:	£103.95
Burgh Castle	Overnight cost per metre:	£0.71
Nr Great Yarmouth	Number of berths:	70
Norfolk	Maximum length:	23
NR31 9PZ	Tidal access:	All states
tel 01493 780331		

Facilities: [WC] ⚓ ⚓ ⚓ ⚓ ⚓ ⚓ 📙 🛒c 🚗 ⚓ [O]

River Wey Navigation
Pyrford Marina Walton Marine Sales

Lock Lane	Annual cost per metre: £123.00
Pyrford	Overnight cost per metre: £c/m
Woking	Number of berths: 150
Surrey	Maximum length: 22
GU22 8XL	Tidal access: n/a
tel 01932 340739	

Facilities: WC ☂ ☎ ✓ ⛽D ⚡P ⚡N ⊗N ! ⛴ ⚓ 🛒c 🔌 🚗

Swale
Swale Marina

Conyer Wharf	Annual cost per metre: £c/m
Teynham	Overnight cost per metre: £c/m
Sittingbourne	Number of berths: 150
Kent	Maximum length: 25
ME9 9HP	Tidal access: HW±2
tel 01795 521562	

Facilities: ☺ WC ☂ ☎ VHF ✓ ⛽D ⚡P ⚡N ⊗P ⊗N ⛴ 🏗 ⚓ 🛒 🔋 🛒c ✂ 🔌 🚗 ⬇v ◻

Thames River
Taplow Investments Ltd

Driftwood, Mill Lane	Annual cost per metre: £166.66
Taplow	Overnight cost per metre: £n/a
Maidenhead	Number of berths: 50
Berkshire	Maximum length: 12
SL6 0AA	Tidal access: n/a
tel 01628 630249	

Facilities: WC ✓ ⚡N ⊗P ⊗N 🏗 🔌 🚗

Thames River
Eel Pie Boatyard Ltd

Eel Pie Island	Annual cost per metre: £105.75
Twickenham	Overnight cost per metre: £n/a
Middlesex	Number of berths: 30
TW1 3DY	Maximum length: 25
tel 0181 892 3626	Tidal access: All states

Facilities: WC ☎ ⚡P ⊗P ⊗N 🏗 🛒 🔋 🔌

2.3 Inland - East

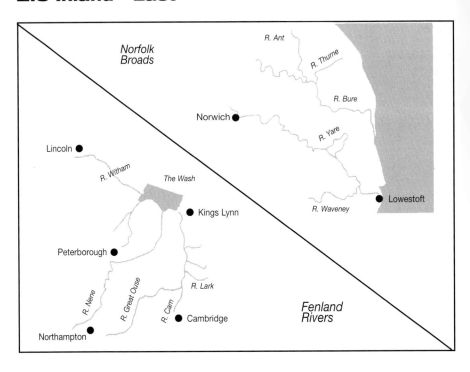

Great Ouse River
Boathaven Littleport

Llyn Road
Littleport
Ely
Cambs
CB6 1QG
tel 01353 863763

Annual cost per metre:	£59.40
Overnight cost per metre:	£0.22
Number of berths:	60
Maximum length:	21
Tidal access:	Non tidal

Facilities: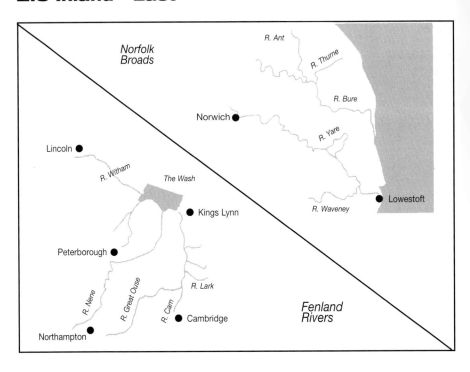

Great Ouse River
Buckden Marina

Mill Road
Buckden
Huntingdon
Cambridgeshire
PE18 9RY
tel 01480 810355

Annual cost per metre:	£94.01
Overnight cost per metre:	£0.55
Number of berths:	260
Maximum length:	11
Tidal access:	Non tidal

Facilities:

Great Ouse River
Crosshall Marine

Crosshall Road	Annual cost per metre:	£103.00
St Neots	Overnight cost per metre:	£0.55
Cambridgeshire	Number of berths:	116
PE19 4AE	Maximum length:	10.6
tel 01480 472763	Tidal access:	Non tidal

Facilities: WC 🛠 🔧 ⛽D 🅿 ⚓ 🔩 🏗 ⚓ 🧺 🔌 🛒 🖼 🚗 ⬆

Great Ouse River
Ely Marina

Waterside	Annual cost per metre:	£98.40
Ely	Overnight cost per metre:	£0.66
Cambs	Number of berths:	200
CB7 4AU	Maximum length:	18
tel 01353 664622	Tidal access:	Non tidal

Facilities: WC 🛠 📞 🔧 ⛽D 🅿P ⚓ 🔩 🔩 🏗 ⚓ 🧺 🖼 🚗 ⬆

Great Ouse River
Hartford Marina

Banks End	Annual cost per metre:	£118.85
Huntingdon	Overnight cost per metre:	£0.55
Cambridgeshire	Number of berths:	200
PE17 2AA	Maximum length:	22
tel 01480 454677	Tidal access:	Non tidal

Facilities: WC 🛠 📞 VHF 🔧 ⛽D 🔩P ⚓P ⚓N ⚓P ⚓N ! 🔩 🏗 ⚓ 🔌 🛒 🖼 🚗 ⬆ ⊙

Great Ouse River
Hermitage Marina

Earith Bridge	Annual cost per metre:	£68.89
Earith	Overnight cost per metre:	£0.17
Huntingdon	Number of berths:	75
Cambs	Maximum length:	12
PE17 3PR	Tidal access:	Non tidal
tel 01487 840994		

Facilities: WC 🔧 ⛽D 🔩P ⚓N ⚓N ! 🔩 🏗 🧺 🔌 🛒 🖼 🚗 ⬆

Great Ouse River
L H Jones & Son

The Boathaven	Annual cost per metre:	£112.50
Low Rd	Overnight cost per metre:	£0.33
St Ives	Number of berths:	120
Cambridgeshire	Maximum length:	14.5
PE17 4ET	Tidal access:	Non tidal
tel 01480 494040		

Facilities: WC 🛠 📞 🔧 ⛽D 🔩P ⚓P ⚓N 🔩 ⚓ 🧺 🛒 🖼 🚗 ⬆

Great Ouse River
Priory Marina Ltd

Barkers Lane	Annual cost per metre:	£88.59
Bedford	Overnight cost per metre:	£c/m
Beds	Number of berths:	150
MK41 9RL	Maximum length:	21.3
tel 01234 351931	Tidal access:	Non tidal

Facilities: ⬛ 🛟 ⚓ ⛽ 🅿 🅿 ⚓ ⚓ ⚓ ⚓ ❗ 🔧 ⚓ ⚓ 🏪 🍺 ☕ 🅰 🚗 🛟 ◻

Great Ouse River
River Mill Marina

School Lane	Annual cost per metre:	£90.00
Eaton Socon	Overnight cost per metre:	£0.33
St. Neots	Number of berths:	100
Cambs	Maximum length:	21
PE19 3HN	Tidal access:	Non tidal
tel 01480 473456		

Facilities: ⬛ 🛟 ⚓ ⚓ ⛽ ⚓ ⚓ ❗ ⚓ ⚓ 🏪 🍺 ☕ ✂ 🅰 🚗 🛟

Great Ouse River
St Neots Marina

South Street	Annual cost per metre:	£89.08
Eynesbury	Overnight cost per metre:	£0.39
St Neots	Number of berths:	100
Cambs	Maximum length:	10
PE19 2BW	Tidal access:	Non tidal
tel 01480 472411		

Facilities: ⬛ 🛟 ⚓ ⛽ ⚓ ⚓ ⚓ 🏪 ☕ 🅰 🚗 🛟

Great Ouse River
Twenty Pence Marina

Twenty Pence Road	Annual cost per metre:	£60.00
Wilburton	Overnight cost per metre:	£0.20
Ely	Number of berths:	60
Cambs	Maximum length:	25
CB6 3PX	Tidal access:	Non tidal
tel 01954 251118		

Facilities: ⬛ ⚓ ⚓ 🔧 ⚓ 🚗 🛟

Great Ouse River
Westview Marina

High Street	Annual cost per metre:	£68.00
Earith	Overnight cost per metre:	£0.44
Huntingdon	Number of berths:	55
Cambridgeshire	Maximum length:	17
PE17 3PN	Tidal access:	Non tidal
tel 01487 841627		

Facilities: ⬛ 🛟 ⚓ ⛽ ⚓ ⚓ ⚓ ⚓ 🏪 ☕ 🅰 🚗 🛟 ◻

Nene
Billing Aquadrome Marina

Billing Aquadrome	Annual cost per metre:	£57.00
Gt Billing	Overnight cost per metre:	£1.10
Northampton	Number of berths:	120
Northamptonshire	Maximum length:	10
NN3 9DA	Tidal access:	n/a
tel 01604 408312		

Facilities: ᵂᶜ 𝄃 ⚓ 🔧 🛠ₚ ♿ₚ ⚓ 🔌 🛒c 🗝 🚗 ⬇ᵛ ▣

River Bure
Brundall Bay Marina

Riverside	Annual cost per metre:	£122.00
Brundall	Overnight cost per metre:	£c/m
Norwich	Number of berths:	177
Norfolk	Maximum length:	14
NR13 5PN	Tidal access:	c/m
tel 01603 716606		

Facilities: ᵂᶜ 𝄃 🔧 ⛽ᴅ 🛠ₚ ♿ₚ ⚓ 🏗 ⚓ 🛒 🗝 🚗 ⬇ᵛ

River Bure
Horning Ferry Marina

Ferry Road	Annual cost per metre:	£n/a
Horning	Overnight cost per metre:	£n/a
Norwich	Number of berths:	80
Norfolk	Maximum length:	15
NR12 8PS	Tidal access:	All states
tel 01692 630392		

Facilities: ᵂᶜ 𝄃 ⚓ 🔧 ⛽ᴅ ⛽ₚ 🛠ɴ ♿ɴ ❗ 🏗 🛒 🔌 🗝 🚗 ⬇ᵛ ▣

River Lark
Isleham Marina Ltd

Fenbank	Annual cost per metre:	£50.00
Isleham	Overnight cost per metre:	£c/m
Ely	Number of berths:	50
Cambs	Maximum length:	20
CB7 5SL	Tidal access:	n/a
tel 01638 780663		

Facilities: ᵂᶜ 🛠ₚ 🛠ɴ ♿ɴ ⚓ ⚓ 🛒 🚗 ⬇ᵛ

River Nene
Mill Marina

Midland Road	Annual cost per metre:	£55.50
Thrapston	Overnight cost per metre:	£c/m
Kettering	Number of berths:	30
Northants	Maximum length:	24
NN14 4JR	Tidal access:	none
tel 01832 732850		

Facilities: ᵂᶜ 𝄃 ⚓ 🔧 🛠ₚ ♿ₚ ♿ɴ ⚓ 🛒 🔌 🚗 ⬇ᵛ ▣

River Nene
Oundle Marina

Barnwell Road
Oundle
Peterborough
Cambridgeshire
PE8 5PA
tel 01832 272762

Annual cost per metre:	£48.00
Overnight cost per metre:	£0.50
Number of berths:	200
Maximum length:	19
Tidal access:	n/a

Facilities: ⬚ ⬚ ⬚ ⬚ ⬚ ⬚ ⬚ ⬚ ⬚ ⬚ ⬚ ⬚ ⬚ ⬚ ⬚ ⬚ ⬚

River Waveney
Waveney River Centre

Burgh St Peter Staithe
Burgh St Peter
Norfolk
NR34 0BT
tel 01502 677217

Annual cost per metre:	£112.16
Overnight cost per metre:	£0.50
Number of berths:	170
Maximum length:	17
Tidal access:	All states

Facilities: ⬚ ⬚ ⬚ ⬚ ⬚ ⬚ ⬚ ⬚ ⬚ ⬚ ⬚ ⬚ ⬚ ⬚ ⬚ ⬚ ⬚ ⬚

River Witham
Boston Marina

5-7 Witham Bank East
Boston
Lincolnshire
PE21 9JU
tel 01205 364420

Annual cost per metre:	£38.00
Overnight cost per metre:	£0.44
Number of berths:	47
Maximum length:	15
Tidal access:	HW±2

Facilities: ⬚ ⬚ VHF ⬚ ⬚ ⬚ ⬚ ⬚ ⬚ ⬚ ⬚

River Witham & Fossdyke
Lincoln Marina

James Kendall & Co Ltd
The Boatyard
Brayford Pool
Lincolnshire
LN1 1RE
tel 01522 526896

Annual cost per metre:	£68.61
Overnight cost per metre:	£0.44
Number of berths:	100
Maximum length:	14
Tidal access:	n\a

Facilities: ⬚ ⬚ ⬚ ⬚ ⬚ ⬚ ⬚ ⬚ ⬚ ⬚ ⬚ ⬚ ⬚ ⬚ ⬚ ⬚ ⬚

River Yare
Bells Dyke

Waterside
Brundal
Norwich
Norfolk
NR13 5PY
tel 01603 713109

Annual cost per metre:	£47.00
Overnight cost per metre:	£0.67l
Number of berths:	50
Maximum length:	12.2
Tidal access:	All states

Facilities: ⬚ ⬚ ⬚

River Yare
Bells Marina

Waterside	Annual cost per metre:	£90.47
Brundall	Overnight cost per metre:	£0.67
Norwich	Number of berths:	73
Norfolk	Maximum length:	18.3
NR13 5PY	Tidal access:	All states
tel 01603 713109		

Facilities: ᵂᶜ 〔 ⚲ₚ ⊗ₚ 🏢 🛒 🔲 🚗 ⬇ᵛ

River Yare
Brooms

Riverside	Annual cost per metre:	£95.00
Brundall	Overnight cost per metre:	£0.55
Norwich	Number of berths:	100
Norfolk	Maximum length:	15
NR13 5PX	Tidal access:	All states
tel 01603 712334		

Facilities: ᵂᶜ 🌿 〔 ⛽ᴅ ⛽ₚ ⚲ₚ ⊗ₚ ! 🏢 ⬇ 🛒 🔌 🛒ᶜ 🔲 🚗 ⬇ᵛ

2.4 Inland - West

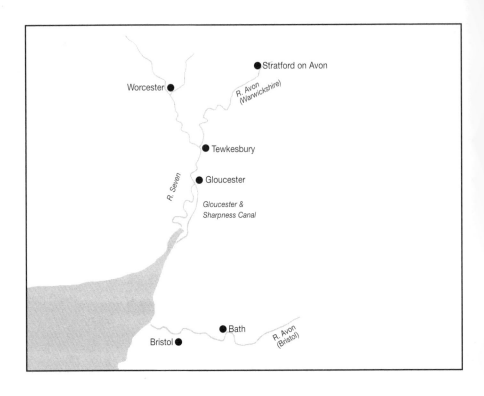

Gloucester & Sharpness Canal
Gloucester Docks

Gloucester
Gloucestershire
GL1 2EJ
tel 01452 318000

Annual cost per metre:	£79.69
Overnight cost per metre:	£c/m
Number of berths:	63
Maximum length:	n/a
Tidal access:	Non tidal

Facilities: WC VHF N P N !

Kennet & Avon Canal
Hilperton Marina

Hilperton Wharf
Hammond Way
Trowbridge
Wiltshire
BA14 8RS
tel 01225 765243

Annual cost per metre:	£75.20
Overnight cost per metre:	£0.24
Number of berths:	100
Maximum length:	30
Tidal access:	Non tidal

Facilities: WC D P N P N !

River Avon (Avon)
Bath Marina

Brassmill Lane	Annual cost per metre:	£106.35
Bath	Overnight cost per metre:	£0.55
Somerset	Number of berths:	55
BA1 3JT	Maximum length:	15.2
tel 01225 424301	Tidal access:	Non tidal

Facilities: 🚾 ⌂ (✎ 🅟ᴅ ⁄ᴘ ⊛ᴘ ! ◀ 🛒 🗳 🛒c 📺 🚗 ⬇ᵛ ⊙ ♿

River Avon (Avon)
Portavon Marina

Bitton Road	Annual cost per metre:	£c/m
Keynsham	Overnight cost per metre:	£c/m
Bristol	Number of berths:	100
Avon	Maximum length:	18.3
BS18 2DD	Tidal access:	Non tidal
tel 0117 986 1626		

Facilities: 🚾 ⌂ 🅟ᴅ ⁄ᴘ ⊛ᴘ ◀ 🏛 ⬆ 🛒 🗳 🛒c 📺 🚗 ⬇ᵛ

River Avon (Avon)
Saltford Marina

The Shallows	Annual cost per metre:	£117.50
Saltford	Overnight cost per metre:	£0.65
Nr Bristol	Number of berths:	100
Avon	Maximum length:	22
BS18 3EZ	Tidal access:	Non tidal
tel 01225 872226		

Facilities: 🚾 ⌂ (✎ 🅟ᴅ ⁄ᴘ ⊛ᴘ ! ◀ 🏛 ⬆ 🛒 🗳 🛒c 📺 🚗 ⬇ᵛ

River Avon (Warwickshire)
Evesham Marina

Kings Road	Annual cost per metre:	£78.75
Evesham	Overnight cost per metre:	£0.37
Worcs	Number of berths:	53
WR11 5BU	Maximum length:	20
tel 01386 48906	Tidal access:	All states

Facilities: 🚾 (🅟ᴅ ⁄ɴ ⊛ɴ ! ◀ 🏛 🛒 📺 🚗 ⬇ᵛ

River Avon (Warwickshire)
Sankey Marine

Worcester Road	Annual cost per metre:	£114.26
Evesham	Overnight cost per metre:	£0.33
Worcs	Number of berths:	60
WR11 4TA	Maximum length:	15
tel 01386 442338	Tidal access:	All states

Facilities: 🚾 ⌂ 🅟ᴅ ⊛ᴘ ◀ 🏛 🗳 🛒c 📺 🚗 ⬇ᵛ

River Severn
Seaborne Yacht Co Ltd

Court Meadow	Annual cost per metre:	£n/a
Kempsey	Overnight cost per metre:	£n/a
Worcestershire	Number of berths:	n/a
tel 01905 820295	Maximum length:	n/a
	Tidal access:	n/a

Facilities: 🆆 📍 ☎ ⚓ ⛽ ⚡ ⚡ 🅿 ! ⛵ ⚓ 🛒 🍺 🚗 🛟 ⊙

River Severn
Severn Valley Boat Centre

The Boat Shop	Annual cost per metre:	£75.00
Mart Lane	Overnight cost per metre:	£1.00
Stourport on Severn	Number of berths:	70
Worcestershire	Maximum length:	21
DY13 9ER	Tidal access:	All states
tel 01299 871165		

Facilities: 🆆 📍 ☎ ⛽ ⚡ 🅿 ! ⚓ 🛒 🍺 🚗 🛟

River Severn
Stourport Marina

Sandy Lane	Annual cost per metre:	£145.00
Stourport on Severn	Overnight cost per metre:	£0.66
Worcestershire	Number of berths:	160
DY13 9QF	Maximum length:	n/a
tel 01299 827082	Tidal access:	n/a

Facilities: 🆆 📍 ☎ ⚓ ⛽ ⚡ 🅿 ! ⛵ ⚓ 🛒 🍺 🚗

River Severn
Upton Marina

Upton Upon Severn	Annual cost per metre:	£159.80
Worcester	Overnight cost per metre:	£1.00
Worcs	Number of berths:	300
WR8 0PB	Maximum length:	22
tel 01684 594287	Tidal access:	Non tidal

Facilities: 🆆 📍 ⚓ ⛽ ⚡ ⚡ 🅿 🅿 ! ⛵ ⚓ 🛒 🍺 ✂ 🚗 🛟 ♿

Rivers Avon (Warwickshire) and Severn
Tewkesbury Marina

Bredon Road	Annual cost per metre:	£134.00
Tewkesbury	Overnight cost per metre:	£0.55
Gloucestershire	Number of berths:	320
GL20 5BY	Maximum length:	22
tel 01684 293737	Tidal access:	n/a

Facilities: 🆆 📍 ☎ VHF ⚓ ⛽ ⛽ ⚡ 🅿 ! ⛵ ⚓ 🛒 🍺 🚗 🛟

Stratford Canal and Upper Avon River
Stratford Marina Ltd

The Boatyard	Annual cost per metre:	£99.29
Clopton Bridge	Overnight cost per metre:	£4.00
Stratford Upon Avon	Number of berths:	10
Warwickshire	Maximum length:	21.5
CV37 6YY	Tidal access:	n/a
tel 01789 269669		

Facilities: [WC] (℗ꜰᴅ ⚲ɴ ⊗ɴ ! ⚓ 🛒 🛒ᴄ 🔃 🚗 ⬇ᵛ

Worcester Birmingham Canal
Droitwich Boat Centre

Hanbury Whay	Annual cost per metre:	£110.93
Hanbury Rd	Overnight cost per metre:	£n/a
Droitwich	Number of berths:	60
Worcs	Maximum length:	n/a
WR9 7DU	Tidal access:	n/a
tel 01905 771018		

Facilities: [WC] ℗ (℗ᴅ ⚲ᴘ ⚲ɴ ⊗ᴘ ⊗ɴ ⚓ ▯ ⚓ 🛒 🛒ᴄ 🔃 🚗 ⬇ᵛ

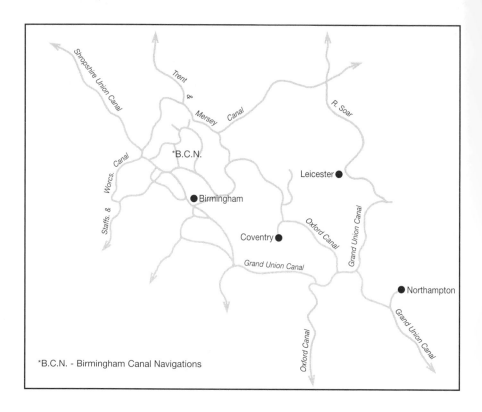

*B.C.N. - Birmingham Canal Navigations

Beeston Canal
Nottingham Castle Marina

Castle Marina Park
Castle Boulevard
Nottingham
Nottinghamshire
NG7 1FD
tel 01602 412672

Annual cost per metre:	£c/m
Overnight cost per metre:	£c/m
Number of berths:	200
Maximum length:	n/a
Tidal access:	Non tidal

Facilities: WC ... VHF ...

Grand Union Canal
Braunston Marina Ltd

The Wharf
Braunston
Nr Daventry
Northants
NN11 7JH
tel 01788 891373

Annual cost per metre:	£94.52
Overnight cost per metre:	£0.46
Number of berths:	240
Maximum length:	22
Tidal access:	Non tidal

Facilities: WC ...

Grand Union Canal
Calcutt Marina

Tomlow Road	Annual cost per metre:	£c/m
Stockton	Overnight cost per metre:	£c/m
Rugby	Number of berths:	100
Warwickshire	Maximum length:	20
CV23 8HX	Tidal access:	Non tidal
tel 01926 813757		

Facilities: 🚾 📞 ⚓ ⛽D ⚓P ⚓N ⊗P ⊗N ! ◀ 🏗 🛒 🛒c 📇 🚗 ⬇v

Grand Union Canal
Cosgrove Marina

The Lock House	Annual cost per metre:	£66.67
Lock Lane, Cosgrove	Overnight cost per metre:	£0.40
Milton Keynes	Number of berths:	110
Bucks	Maximum length:	22
MK19 7JD	Tidal access:	Non tidal
tel 01908 562467		

Facilities: 🚾 📞 ⛽D ⊗N ! 🏗 ⬇ 🛒 🛒c 📇 🚗 ⬇v

Grand Union Canal
Cowroast Marina

Cowroast	Annual cost per metre:	£34.67
Tring	Overnight cost per metre:	£0.90
Herts	Number of berths:	110
HP23 5RE	Maximum length:	22
tel 01448 823222	Tidal access:	Non tidal

Facilities: 🚾 📷 ⛽D ⚓P ⊗P ! ◀ 🏗 ⬇ 🛒 🛒c 📇 🚗 ⬇v ⬜

Grand Union Canal
Harefield Marina

Moorhall Road	Annual cost per metre:	£84.22
Harefield	Overnight cost per metre:	£0.83
Uxbridge	Number of berths:	220
Middlesex	Maximum length:	21.8
UB9 6PD	Tidal access:	Non tidal
tel 01895 822036		

Facilities: 🚾 📞 ⚓ ⛽D ⚓N ⊗N ! ◀ 🏗 ⬇ 🛒 🛒 🛒c 📇 🚗 ⬇v

Grand Union Canal
Milton Keynes Marina

Waterside	Annual cost per metre:	£82.72
Peartree Bridge	Overnight cost per metre:	£0.42
Milton Keynes	Number of berths:	100
Bucks	Maximum length:	21.3
MK6 3BX	Tidal access:	Non tidal
tel 01908 672672		

Facilities: 🚾 ⚓ ⛽D ⚓P ⊗P ⊗N ! ◀ 🏗 🛒 🛒 📇 ⬇v ♿

Grand Union Canal
Welton Hythe Marina

Welton	Annual cost per metre:	£62.83
Daventry	Overnight cost per metre:	£1.84
Northants	Number of berths:	100
NN11 5LG	Maximum length:	21.3
tel 01327 843773	Tidal access:	Non tidal

Facilities: 🚽 ⛽ ✂ ⚓ ! 🛒 🛍 🚗

Grand Union Canal
Whilton Marina Ltd

Whilton Locks	Annual cost per metre:	£78.31
Daventry	Overnight cost per metre:	£0.23
Northants	Number of berths:	200
NN11 5NH	Maximum length:	24
tel 01327 84257	Tidal access:	Non tidal

Facilities: ☺ 🚽 ⛽ ! 🛒 🚗 ♿

Grand Union Canal
Willowbridge Marina

Stoke Rd	Annual cost per metre:	£c/m
Bletchley	Overnight cost per metre:	£c/m
Milton Keynes	Number of berths:	40
Buckinghamshire	Maximum length:	21
MK2 3JZ	Tidal access:	Non tidal
tel 01908 643242		

Facilities: 🚽 ⛽ ! 🛒 🚗

Grand Union/Soar Navigation
L R Harris & Son

Old Junction Boatyard	Annual cost per metre:	£42.51
Meadow Lane	Overnight cost per metre:	£4.23
Syston	Number of berths:	100
Leics	Maximum length:	21.3
LE7 1NR	Tidal access:	n/a
tel 0116 269 2135		

Facilities: 🚽 ⛽ 🛒 🚗

Oxford Canal
Fenny Marina

Fenny Compton	Annual cost per metre:	£102.88
Leamington Spa	Overnight cost per metre:	£1.33
Warwicks	Number of berths:	100
CV33 0XD	Maximum length:	c/m
tel 01295 770461	Tidal access:	n/a

Facilities: 🚽 ⛽ ! 🛒

River Soar
East Midlands Boat Services

Willow Moorings	Annual cost per metre:	£85.00
London Road	Overnight cost per metre:	£0.66
Kegworth	Number of berths:	60
Derby	Maximum length:	22
DE74 2EY	Tidal access:	Non tidal
tel 01509 672385		

Facilities: 🅿ᴅ ⚡ɴ ⊛ɴ ! ⛴ 🧺ᴄ 🔲 🚗 ⬇ᵛ

River Soar
Nimbus Narrow Boats

The Boat Yard	Annual cost per metre:	£57.50
Mill Lane	Overnight cost per metre:	£c/m
Thurmaston, Leicester	Number of berths:	20
Leicestershire	Maximum length:	20
LE4 8AF	Tidal access:	Non tidal
tel 01162 693069		

Facilities: ᵂᶜ ✔ 🅿ᴅ ⚡ɴ ⊛ɴ ! ⛴ 🧺 🧺ᴄ 🔲 🚗 ⬇ᵛ

River Soar
Red Hill Marina

Red Hill	Annual cost per metre:	£c/m
Ratcliffe On Soar	Overnight cost per metre:	£c/m
Nottingham	Number of berths:	400
Notts	Maximum length:	21.3
NG11 0EB	Tidal access:	All states
tel 01509 672770		

Facilities: ᵂᶜ 🅿ᴅ ⚡ɴ ⊛ɴ ! ⛴ 🏗 🧺ᴄ 🔲 🚗 ⬇ᵛ

River Soar
Sileby Mill Boatyard

Mill Lane	Annual cost per metre:	£52.00
Sileby	Overnight cost per metre:	£1.50
Loughborough	Number of berths:	75
Leics	Maximum length:	22
LE12 7NF	Tidal access:	n/a
tel 01509 813583		

Facilities: ᵂᶜ 📠 ☎ 🅿ᴅ ⚡ᴘ ⚡ɴ ⊛ɴ ! ⛴ ⚓ 🧺 🧺ᴄ 🔲 🚗 ⬇ᵛ ⬛

River Trent
Beeston Marina

Riverside Road	Annual cost per metre:	£68.55
Beeston	Overnight cost per metre:	£1.50
Nottingham	Number of berths:	100
Notts	Maximum length:	24
NG9 1NA	Tidal access:	All states
tel 0115 922 3168		

Facilities: ᵂᶜ 📠 ☎ 🅿ᴅ 🅿ᴘ ⊛ɴ ! ⛴ 🏗 🧺 🛢 🧺ᴄ 🔲 🚗 ⬇ᵛ

Shropshire Union Canal
Barbridge Marina

Wardle	Annual cost per metre:	£65.17
Nantwich	Overnight cost per metre:	£3.00
Cheshire	Number of berths:	100
CW5 6BE	Maximum length:	n/a
tel 01270 528682	Tidal access:	n/a

Facilities: ☺ 🆆 ⚓ ⚓N ⊗N ⚓ ⚓ 🧺 🧺c 🎴 🚗 ⛵

Staffs & Worcs Canal
Calf Heath Marina

Kings Road	Annual cost per metre:	£47.10
Calf Heath	Overnight cost per metre:	£c/m
Wolverhampton	Number of berths:	10
West Midlands	Maximum length:	24
WV10 7DU	Tidal access:	All states
tel 01902 790570		

Facilities: 🆆 ☎ ⛽D ⚓N ⊗N ! ⚓ 🏠 🍺 🎴 🚗 ⛵ ♿

Trent & Mersey Canal
Shobnall Marina

Shobnall Road	Annual cost per metre:	£68.15
Burton on Trent	Overnight cost per metre:	£c/m
Staffordshire	Number of berths:	60
DE14 2AU	Maximum length:	23.3
tel 01283 542718	Tidal access:	All states

Facilities: 🆆 ⚓ ⛽D ⚓P ⊗P ! ⚓ 🏠 🧺 🍺 🧺c 🎴 🚗 ⛵

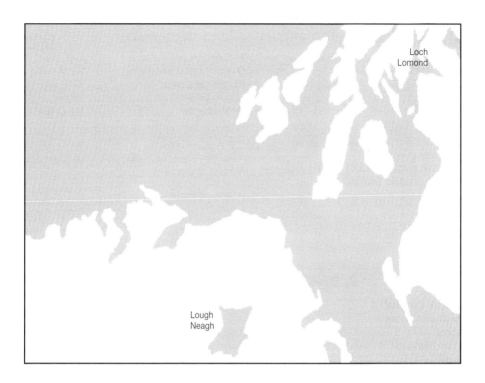

Caledonian Canal
Caley Marina

Canal Road	Annual cost per metre:	£78.00
Muirtown	Overnight cost per metre:	£c/m
Inverness	Number of berths:	50
Inverness-shire, Scotland	Maximum length:	45
IV3 6NF	Tidal access:	HW±4
tel 01463 236539		

Facilities:

Caledonian Canal
Seaport Marina

British Waterways Caledonian Canal	Annual cost per metre:	£97.58
Muirtown Wharf	Overnight cost per metre:	£c/m
Muirtown	Number of berths:	40
Inverness	Maximum length:	45.7
IV3 5LE	Tidal access:	HW±4
tel 01463 233140		

Facilities: ☺ WC 👣 📞 VHF ⛽D 🛢P 🛢N ⊗P ⊗N ! 🧺 🛒c 🔁 🚗 ⬇v ☐

Crinan Canal
Bellanoch Marina

British Waterways Canal Office
Pier Square
Ardrishaig
Argyll
PA30 8DZ
tel 01546 603210

Annual cost per metre:	£101.80
Overnight cost per metre:	£2.25
Number of berths:	67
Maximum length:	26.8
Tidal access:	Non tidal

Facilities: [WC] ⬅ VHF ⊞D ⊗P 🧺 🧺c 🚠 🚗 ⬇v ♿

Leven River/Loch Lomond
Loch Lomond Marina

Riverside
Balloch
Alexandria
Dunbartonshire
G83 8LF
tel 01389 752069

Annual cost per metre:	£127.83
Overnight cost per metre:	£c/m
Number of berths:	45
Maximum length:	10
Tidal access:	n/a

Facilities: [WC] ⬅ ✦ ⊞D ⊞P ⚓N ⊗N ⛵ ⚓ 🧺 🧺c 🚠 🚗 ⬇v

Loch Lomond
Ardlui Marina

Ardlui
Loch Lomond
Argyll
Scotland
G83 7EB
tel 01301 704243

Annual cost per metre:	£130.00
Overnight cost per metre:	£1.00
Number of berths:	100
Maximum length:	14
Tidal access:	n/a

Facilities: [WC] ⬅ ☎ VHF ⊞D ⊞P ⚓P ⊗P ! ⛵ 🔧 🧺 ⛽ 🚗 ⬇v ⊡

Lough Neagh
Ballyronan Marina

99 Shore Road
Ballyronan
Magherafelt
Londonderry
BT45 6JG
tel 01648 762205

Annual cost per metre:	£34.50
Overnight cost per metre:	£0.28
Number of berths:	36
Maximum length:	n/a
Tidal access:	Non tidal

Facilities: [WC] ⊗N ⛵ 🧺 ⬇v

Lough Neagh
Kinnego Marina

Marina Office
Oxford Island
Lurgon
Co. Armagh
BT66 6NJ
tel 01762 327573

Annual cost per metre:	£n/a
Overnight cost per metre:	£c/m
Number of berths:	84
Maximum length:	12
Tidal access:	Non tidal

Facilities: [WC] ⬅ ☎ VHF ⊞D ⊞P ⚓N ⊗P ⛵ 🔧 🧺 ⛽ 🧺c 🚠 🚗 ⬇v ⊡

3.1 France
Index to French Marinas

3.1 France

Brest

Port De Plaisance Du Moulin Blanc	Annual cost for a 9m boat: F8187,00
29200 Brest	Overnight cost for a 9m boat: F107,00
Bureau Du Port	Number of berths: 1325
tel 02 98 02 20 02	Maximum length: 30
	Tidal access: All states

Facilities: WC 🅿 📞 VHF ⛽ 🅿 🛥 🛥 ⊗ ⊗ 🏊 ⚓ ⚓ 🛒 🍺 🏪 ✂ 🚉 🚗 🛗 🅾

Morlaix

Port De Plaisance De Morlaix	Annual cost for a 9m boat: F3726,00
Le Styvel. Cours Beaumont	Overnight cost for a 9m boat: F71,00
29600 Morlaix	Number of berths: 200
tel 02 98 62 13 14	Maximum length: 14
	Tidal access: HW+1-1.5

Facilities: WC 🅿 📞 VHF ⛽ 🛥 🛥 ⊗ ⊗ 🏊 ⚓ ⚓ 🛒 🍺 🏪 🚉 🚗 🛗

Trebeurden

Port de Plaisance de Trebeurden	Annual cost for a 9m boat: F7000,00
Parking du Castel	Overnight cost for a 9m boat: F115,00
BP40	Number of berths: 500
22560 Trebeurden	Maximum length: 16
tel 02 96 23 64 00	Tidal access: HW±9

Facilities: WC 🅿 📞 VHF ⚓ ⛽ 🅿 🛥 ⊗ 🏊 ⚓ ⚓ 🛒 🍺 🏪 ✂ 🚉 🚗 🛗 🅾

Perros Guirec

Perros Guirec	Annual cost for a 9m boat: Fc/m
Capitainerie	Overnight cost for a 9m boat: Fc/m
17 Rue Anatole Le Braz	Number of berths: 680
22700 Perros-Guirec	Maximum length: 20
tel 02 96 49 80 50	Tidal access: HW±1

Facilities: WC 🅿 📞 VHF ⛽ 🅿 🛥 🛥 ⊗ ⊗ 🏊 ⚓ 🛒 🍺 🏪 ✂ 🚉 🅾

Treguier

Port De Treguier	Annual cost for a 9m boat: Fc/m
Bureau de Port de Plaisance	Overnight cost for a 9m boat: Fc/m
22220 Treguier	Number of berths: 320
tel 02 96 92 42 37	Maximum length: 12
	Tidal access: All states

Facilities: WC 🅿 📞 VHF ⛽ 🛥 ⊗ 🏊 ⚓ 🛒 🍺 🏪 🚉 🅾

Port de Lezardrieux

Port De Lezardrieux	Annual cost for a 9m boat: F5364,00
Bureau de Port	Overnight cost for a 9m boat: F101,00
22740 Lezardrieux	Number of berths: 650
tel 02 96 20 14 22	Maximum length: 20
	Tidal access: All States

Facilities: WC 🅿 📞 VHF ⚓ ⛽ 🅿 🛥 🛥 ⊗ ⊗ 🏊 ⚓ ⚓ 🛒 🍺 🏪 ✂ 🚉 🚗 🛗 🅾

Paimpol

Port De Plaisance De Paimpol	Annual cost for a 9m boat: F4424,00
Quai Neuf	Overnight cost for a 9m boat: F106,00
Maison des Plaisanciers	Number of berths: 305
22500 Piampol	Maximum length: 40
tel 02 96 20 47 65	Tidal access: HW±2

Facilities: WC 📻 ☎ ⛽D ⚓P ⛽P 🛒 🏠 🍺 🧺c ✂ 🔧

St Quay Portrieux

St Quay - Port d'Armor	Annual cost for a 9m boat: F72,00
Capitainerie	Overnight cost for a 9m boat: F118,00
Esplanade Du Port	Number of berths: 850
22410 St Quay Portrieux	Maximum length: 25
tel 02 96 70 81 30	Tidal access: All states

Facilities: WC 📻 ☎ VHF ⛽D ⛽P ⚓P ⚓N 🏠 🛒 🍺 🧺c 🔧 🚗 ⛽V 🅾

Port of Binic

Binic	Annual cost for a 9m boat: F5154,75
Bureau du Port	Overnight cost for a 9m boat: F81,00
Quai Jean Bart	Number of berths: 320
22520 Binic	Maximum length: 15
tel 02 96 73 61 86	Tidal access: c/m

Facilities: WC 📻 ☎ VHF ⚓P ⚓N ⛽P ⛽N 🏠 ⚓ 🛒 🍺 🧺c ✂ 🔧 🅾

Dahouet

Port de Dahouet	Annual cost for a 9m boat: F7000,00
Capitainerie Port De Dahouet	Overnight cost for a 9m boat: F82,00
Quai des Salines	Number of berths: 500
22370 Pleneuf-Val-Andre	Maximum length: 15
tel 02 96 72 82 85	Tidal access: HW+2.5

Facilities: WC 📻 ☎ VHF ⚓P ⛽P 🏠 🍺 🧺c ✂ 🔧 🚗

St Malo

Port De Plaisance Des Sablons	Annual cost for a 9m boat: F10108,00
Bureau de Port	Overnight cost for a 9m boat: F120,00
Terre-Plein Sud	Number of berths: 1216
35400 Saint Malo	Maximum length: 15
tel 02 99 81 71 34	Tidal access: All states

Facilities: WC 📻 ☎ VHF ⛽D ⛽P ⚓P ⚓N ⛽P ⛽N 🏠 ⚓ 🛒 🍺 🧺c ✂ 🔧

St Malo - Bassin Vauban

St Malo - Bassin Vauban	Annual cost for a 9m boat: F7725,62
Port de Plaisance Vauban	Overnight cost for a 9m boat: F120,00
Bassin Vauban	Number of berths: 225
35400 Saint Malo	Maximum length: unlimited
tel 02 99 56 51 91	Tidal access: HW±5

Facilities: WC 📻 ☎ VHF ⚓P ⛽P 🏠 🍺 🧺c 🔧 🚗 ⛽V 🅾

Port de la Minotais

Port De La Minotais	Annual cost for a 9m boat:	F8100,00
Mairie	Overnight cost for a 9m boat:	F86,00
22490 Plouer/Rance	Number of berths:	240
tel 02 96 86 83 15	Maximum length:	13
	Tidal access:	HW±4

Facilities: WC 🏠 (VHF ⚓P ⊗P ⊼ ⊞ 🧺 🛢 🛒c 🔌 ⚓

Herel

Port de Plaisance de Herel	Annual cost for a 9m boat:	Fn/a
Bureau du Port	Overnight cost for a 9m boat:	F105,00
50400 Granville	Number of berths:	1000
tel 02 33 50 20 06	Maximum length:	15
	Tidal access:	HW-2.5+3.5

Facilities: WC 🏠 (VHF ⛽D ⛽P ⚓P ⊗P ⊼ ⊞ 🧺 🛢 🛒c ✂ 🔌 🚗 ⚓ ☉

Cherbourg

88 Capitainerie	Annual cost for a 9m boat:	F8970,00
50100 Cherbourg	Overnight cost for a 9m boat:	F110,00
tel 02 33 87 65 70	Number of berths:	1300
	Maximum length:	25
	Tidal access:	All states

Facilities: WC 🏠 (VHF ⚓ ⛽D ⛽P ⚓P ⚓N ⊗P ⊗N ⊼ ⊞ ⚓ 🧺 🛢 🛒c ✂ 🔌 🚗 ⚓ ☉

Saint-Vaast

Port Saint-Vaast	Annual cost for a 9m boat:	F7671,00
Place Auguste Contamine	Overnight cost for a 9m boat:	F103,00
50550 Saint Vaast La Hougue	Number of berths:	665
tel 02 33 23 61 00	Maximum length:	20
	Tidal access:	HW-3+2.15

Facilities: WC 🏠 (VHF ⚓ ⛽D ⛽P ⚓P ⊗P ⊼ ⊞ ⚓ 🧺 🛢 🛒c 🔌 🚗 ⚓ ☉

Port Carentan

Port Carentan	Annual cost for a 9m boat:	F4289,00
Rue des Remblais	Overnight cost for a 9m boat:	F81,00
BP 450	Number of berths:	270
50500 Carentan	Maximum length:	35
tel 02 33 42 24 44	Tidal access:	HW-2+3

Facilities: WC 🏠 (VHF ⛽D ⛽P ⚓P ⚓N ⊗P ⊗N ! ⊼ ⊞ 🧺 🛢 🛒c 🔌 🚗 ⚓ ☉

Courseuilles

Port de Courseuilles	Annual cost for a 9m boat:	Fc/m
Quai Ouest	Overnight cost for a 9m boat:	Fc/m
14470 Courseulles sur Mer	Number of berths:	750
tel 02 31 37 51 69	Maximum length:	13
	Tidal access:	HW±2

Facilities: WC 🏠 (VHF ⚓P ⊗P ⊼ ⊞ 🧺 🛢 🛒c 🔌 🚗 ⚓

Ouistreham

Port De Plaisance De Ouistreham
Bassin de Plaisance
14150 Ouistreham
tel 02 31 96 91 37

Annual cost for a 9m boat: F7190,00
Overnight cost for a 9m boat: F119,00
Number of berths: 620
Maximum length: 25
Tidal access: c/m

Facilities: 🆆 📠 📞 VHF 📠ᴅ 📠ᴘ ↗ᴘ ⊛ᴘ ⚓ 🏗 🧺c 🔁 ⬇v

Deauville

Port Deauville
Quai Des Marchands
14800 Deauville
tel 02 31 98 30 01

Annual cost for a 9m boat: Fc/m
Overnight cost for a 9m boat: Fc/m
Number of berths: 700
Maximum length: 35
Tidal access: HW±4

Facilities: 🆆 📠 📞 VHF ↗ 📠ᴅ ↗ᴘ ⊛ᴘ 🏗 ⚓ 🧺 🔌 🧺c 🚗 ⬇v

Deauville - Bassin Mornay

Deauville - Bassin Mornay
Port Public de Deauville
Mairie de Deauville
14800 Deauville
tel 02 31 98 30 01

Annual cost for a 9m boat: Fc/m
Overnight cost for a 9m boat: Fc/m
Number of berths: 700
Maximum length: 30
Tidal access: HW±4

Facilities: 🆆 📠 📞 VHF ↗ 📠ᴅ ↗ᴘ ⊛ᴘ ⚓ 🏗 🧺 🔌 🧺c ✂ 🔁 🚗 ⬇v 🅾

Honfleur

Cercle Nautique de Honfleur
8 Rue St Antoine
BP 118
14600 Honfleur
tel 02 31 98 87 13

Annual cost for a 9m boat: Fn/a
Overnight cost for a 9m boat: F95,00
Number of berths: 73
Maximum length: 14
Tidal access: All states

Facilities: 🆆 📠 ↗ᴘ ⊛ᴘ ⚓ 🏗 🧺 🔌 🧺c 🔁

Le Harve

Le Harve Plaisance
Port de Plaisance
Boulevard Clemenceau
76600 Le Harve
tel 02 35 21 23 95

Annual cost for a 9m boat: Fc/m
Overnight cost for a 9m boat: Fc/m
Number of berths: 1080
Maximum length: 20
Tidal access: All states

Facilities: 🆆 📠 📞 VHF ↗ 📠ᴅ 📠ᴘ ↗ᴘ ⊛ᴘ ⚓ 🏗 🧺 🔌 🧺c ✂ 🔁 ⬇v 🅾

Fecamp

Port De Plaisance De Fecamp
Chaussee Des Freres Levasseur
76400 Fecamp
tel 02 35 28 13 58

Annual cost for a 9m boat: Fc/m
Overnight cost for a 9m boat: Fc/m
Number of berths: 580
Maximum length: 18
Tidal access: All states

Facilities: 🆆 📠 📞 VHF 📠ᴅ ↗ᴘ ⊛ᴘ ⚓ 🏗 🧺 🧺c 🔁 🚗 ⬇v

Saint Valery en Caux

Saint Valery en Caux
Capitainerie Du Port
76460 St Valery En Caux
tel 02 35 97 01 30

Annual cost for a 9m boat:	F8670,00
Overnight cost for a 9m boat:	F100,00
Number of berths:	600
Maximum length:	25
Tidal access:	HW±2.15

Facilities: WC ⌐ ☏ VHF ▮D ▮P ⁄P ⁄N ⊗P ⊗N ! ⤒ 𝕀 ⤓ 🧺 ▯ ⓦc ✂ 🚗 ↡ ▢

Jehan Ango

Port Jehan Ango
Pont Jehan Ango
76200 Dieppe
tel 02 35 40 19 79

Annual cost for a 9m boat:	F12300,00
Overnight cost for a 9m boat:	F135,00
Number of berths:	450
Maximum length:	27
Tidal access:	All states

Facilities: WC ⌐ ☏ VHF ⌁ ▮D ▮P ⁄P ⊗P ⤒ 𝕀 🧺 ▯ ⓦc 🔲 🚗 ↡ ▢

Calais Marina

Calais Marina
Basin Ouest
62100 Calais
tel 03 21 34 55 23

Annual cost for a 9m boat:	F3454,78
Overnight cost for a 9m boat:	F52,00
Number of berths:	132
Maximum length:	50
Tidal access:	c/m

Facilities: WC ⌐ ☏ ▮D ⁄P ⊗P 𝕀 ⤓ 🧺 ▯ 🚗 ↡

Dunkerque

Yacht Club De La Mer Du Nord
Quai Des Monitors
59140 Dunkerque
tel 03 28 66 79 90

Annual cost for a 9m boat:	F6500,00
Overnight cost for a 9m boat:	F108,00
Number of berths:	250
Maximum length:	30
Tidal access:	c/m

Facilities: WC ⌐ ☏ VHF ⌁ ▮D ▮P ⁄P ⊗P ⤒ 𝕀 🧺 ▯ ⓦc ✂ 🔲 🚗 ↡ ▢